The Commercial and Industrial Roof Repair Field Guide

Strategies, Theories and Proper Search Techniques

2014-2015

J. L. Foster

AuthorHouse™ LLC
1663 Liberty Drive
Bloomington, IN 47403
www.authorhouse.com
Phone: 1-800-839-8640

Published by AuthorHouse 02/05/2014

ISBN: 978-1-4918-6108-0 (sc)
ISBN: 978-1-4918-6111-0 (e)

Library of Congress Control Number: 2014902223

Preface to the Repair Personnel

This book is not written in the typical textbook fashion. It is instead written or presented to you in the literal sense as myself have instructed people on the job except, this is much more advanced. If I taught everyone how to do things like me, I would have been out of a job pretty quick. This is that training which everyone else has received plus that of my own understanding and invention brought on by necessity. My employees have never received this specialized training that I have utilized for many years, they just couldn't understand or explain what I was doing or how I did it. Plus it would have taken too long to work through a day-to-day or a person-to-person basis, as you are always on a time limit on every call and you may receive new helpers/employees on a regular basis. Teaching this information on site per person would take an average of about 10 years.

Never asked to be a roof repairman myself. Kinda fell into it. I figured something out one day that the foreman on the job couldn't and the owner sent me out on a repair the next day, needless to say I never stopped. No training on how to find or even where to start searching, and I found that what most people had told me at the time was incorrect or simply crap. People often give wrong information only to see others fail. Its a form of control.

I have spent a majority of my life working for employers who bragged about paying me as little as possible while at the same time charging the customer as much as possible and being offended that I felt other repairmen and myself were grossly under paid and over worked. Employers had a good argument. Roof repairmen have no real specialty, no actual real training and if you don't like it, go get another job, that was their defense. Roof repairmen often get little respect or pay. The money is there, matter of fact there is good money there and unfortunately you like myself only get a percentage of that money only because thats the way it is. For some, a roof repairman position is not a real position, and in many cases it is a part time position. Depending on the size of a town or city a single repairman or two is more than enough to service the whole town, while a big city may employ 200 or more full time repairmen at any given time.

Its been my mission for over 30 years to add validity to the position of a Roof repairman/woman and even the true recognition and justifiable traits of a true roof repair specialist. It can take a whole life time to figure it out in theory all the causes and effects of roof related problems/items and solutions, but with the change of materials and applications such as construction and building codes things and situations change, therefore the experience, training and understanding is lost forever. The old school roofing I learned from men who learned their trade in the early 1940's and they learned their craft from roofers from the early 1910's and them from the late 1890's and so on probably just like you. One thing I have noticed about it all is that many of the roofers and repairmen made little money, got virtually no actual training and pretty much died poor and with many illnesses while the owners lived long and fat.

Things change, people change like myself am different. Making an attempt of removing all the smoke and mirrors, wives tales and down right myths out of a shady and unpredictable so called career was at the very least quite difficult. This is not a scientific diagram of what could or would happen, this is how things happen in the real world of roof repairs. No confusion, no misrepresentation. We are just exposing the facts for what they are out of investigation and relentless need required in figuring out what where when and how roof leaks become active and if we can quickly apply a simple 1-2-3 step program that would fit almost all scenarios as much as possible.

Spending over thirty years in intense emergency, typical and monotonous commercial/industrial roof repair/leak situations of all types, has allowed me to expand the science of roof/non-roof related problems and indicating strategies a bit. They are spread out in a common systematic process that is to be followed for every single commercial or flat roof repair application in the same manner, every time. There are exceptions, those exceptions all that I can find are also covered to the best of my knowledge.

This is the first field guide that teaches the strategy of how to find the problem so a repair can be made, not how to patch it, but where the problem actually originates from so the proper patch of your choice can be made. Kinda like C.S.I., or R.S.I. (Roof Scene Investigation)

Large bars and graphs with huge amounts of learning material just aren't sexy in the roofing world. Repair people are, generally extremely intelligent and have a quick learning curb but get bored easily and most of us lack patience. Were taught to have patience, if your a repair type person, you probably have little patience by nature. This can be a bad thing if not controlled. Guess what? This ia also an admired thing as well. This get up and do attitude can be extremely powerful, don't ever let anyone doubt that or hamper that. Is it being impatient, or is it simply people who just want to get stuff done? This is a very physical, and time consuming profession that requires a go getter. We know what hurry up and wait actually means! For those who do not know what it means, it means I or you are waiting on someone else, and when they finally get the hell out of the way, we can kick some butt, get the job done and go home.

Learning how to put down a patch is actually a secondary thing. Finding the actual problem and being absolutely sure about it is, is the hard part. We want to go to any roof repair call, whether it be an emergency or not, make a positive, permanent and correct roof repair within a reasonable amount of time, every time. Certainly thats not too much to ask. Sometimes just a little hint to push us in the right direction which would make all the difference is all we need.

If everyone solved every roof related problem the first time on every call, would there be any work at all? Yes, there is still plenty of work. We just transfer some of that old budget spent on roof repairs and spend it on maintaining the roof in other ways. Maybe replace sections of the older roof with new roof as the years pass, and that money saved today can be spent tomorrow and we want it spent in a smart way. Our customers trust us with their money after all don't they? Lets spend their money wisely and show them the results. Those results? Stopping roof leaks at a minimum cost and time in a professional and safe manner!

You won't see many "roof repair companies," out there. For the most part there are roofing companies that have a repair division and then most of the time investment is not made in the education or further development of better, quicker more efficient ways to attack certain types of roof related problems or better pay for their employees, it instead goes into the pockets of greedy corporations. Some roofing companies and the fly-by-nighters want the customer to replace the whole roof, and not solve the problem with a two dollar patch. This practice puts repair personnel in a poor light even though the repairman/woman has great intentions of protecting the customers interests. An absolute process will eliminate the conflict while protecting the repairman/woman.

There are those who avoid doing the very best they can and there are those who just can't find anything while doing their very best. Sometimes the best of us have a hard time finding the most difficult roof leak/roof related problem, on the other hand who hasn't had a heck of a time trying to find the most simple roof leak? These are the roof leaks or calls that everyone in the company avoids. The roof leaks everyone wants to stop, but can't get a handle on.

These are not simple roof leaks, these are the roof leaks that have multiple people and roofing companies attending to them regularly at a great expense. If your looking for real solutions to these types of complicated roof related problems and you want to make typical roof repairs a 1-2-3, A-B-C thing, your in the right place.

Just please read this book throughly, then take it on the roof. You do not have to apply anything foreign or learn a whole new language. You will learn new expressions for things you may have already seen but didn't know what they were. Actually, after reading this book you will see things for as they really are, and it is what it is. This book explains how to track the activity from start to finish while eliminating other possibilities. When you understand that, roof repairs? Easy! Not all, but many will become second nature applications. You can have a, "Just another typical day at the office kind of day regardless of the tough circumstances, kind of day everyday."

There is an easy way and a hard way to do things, repairmen and women know that sometimes the best thing to do is the hard thing, and that must be done to solve the problem. We can and will cut down on the chain of events that leads to bad or unproductive time consuming situations and head those problems off at the pass, so to speak as much as possible.

I found that of all the repairmen I have trained over the years, only a very few stayed in the field. Even though they had the best training offered at that time, the work was too much for the pay. Roof repair work is too difficult for the average person or average pay, that's why it takes a certain type of person to stick with it. You have to be pretty strong to stay in the field for one year, let alone 30 plus years like myself, and don't think for a second I take it lightly. Lets be perfectly clear, roofing is one thing, roof repairs are totally another. If you are a repairman/woman you understand my point.

Roof repair work is working on all types of roofs, including shingles under what is almost always difficult weather condition or situations, and this will happen though out the course of a single day. This can happen, all day, every day during bad weather of course. Did I also mention that this happens all the time too if you live in the right part of the world?

This book, will hopefully help legitimize this particular field of commercial and industrial roof repair specialization that should be recognized more as a professional category with a positive and modern image. That change is hard work, dedication and in your hands.

A roof repairman/woman is usually a multi-talented specialist after all who understands many different trades and applications and in most cases; a sheet/metal worker, carpenter, insulation specialist. They will be versed in siding, also concrete, and a roofer. In most cases, a repair person is the laborer as well as back grounds in plumbing, mechanical. Not only are there those trades right off the top almost required, there is the human resource and managerial aspect of dealing with customers, employees and bosses.

Plus! plus, you have to find the actual entry point where the water is getting into the roof at with back figuring how it tracked across the building with imagination and physics while doing this quickly in one trip out, without causing any accidental damage. Don't forget the customer wants it done with no call backs, period! Oh, and your sons basketball game is at 4:30! By the way? Where is my helper? Did he fall of the roof? Many things happen in the course of the day for a repairman/woman. Surprisingly, some have had days much more busier and way more harder than this, some never made it home.

Underlaying all of that is the fact that if you are not only a roof repairman or repair woman, you are also a sales person. Every repair you make and how you make it sells or doesn't sell the next call. If they don't call you back for new things, your probably in trouble.

I have been so frustrated searching out a roof leak that I can't tell you how many times I wanted to just tear off screaming and swearing! Change my name, cut my hair and go to work at a restaurant with the assumed name of Ringo. The aggravation goes beyond anything anyone every told me it would. Sadly enough I have literally broken down in frustration. Not just because I couldn't find a roof leak, but the same repeat roof leak, and it just so happens to be a bad day too! Not often but a couple of times over the many years, I just couldn't take it any more. If you have been a roof repairman/woman for more than a year you know the true feeling of anguish and frustration of not being able to find the entry point(cut/slice on the roof surface) especially when it really matters. The more return calls you make for the same roof leak, the worst it gets.

Plus the stress on the body from extreme weather conditions compounded with exposure to chemicals and the emotional beat down everyday, its a wonder any of us survive more than five years. Some repairmen have literally walked off and never came back. Something that should never be witnessed. How could a person be so absolutely upset and frustrated that they are just walking away from their bread and butter? I have seen it several times. Some of you may have as well. That's how deep the frustration and fear of failing can be.

For myself, unfortunately there was no help for me as there is for you. Walking away a couple a times from this field frustrated, angry and yet I found myself back on the roof. Couldn't let it defeat me. Luckily in retrospect I connected some dots and found some direction. Now you will learn my secrets. I think more about safety now a days. For instance, those smoke stacks pumping hazardous chemicals out of the plant or company/business are most likely falling down on you. For some reason those chemicals are too dangerous for the people down stairs, but not too dangerous for you. That's what I think about more now.

Being a perfectionist, I want it done better than anyone can and will ever do, every time. This is a hard burden. Add the time away from your family, regrets for myself add up high and tall. Like a doctor being on call, being available for emergencies is probably what a lot of you do if you are reading this book, or if you want to be a good roof repairman/woman, that is the sacrifice thats made by all. You have to accept that if this is your profession, won't hurt much now but it may hurt a lot later. Make time for your family when ever possible.

This book will strengthen your success rate and hopefully increase your wages with your understanding of how roof leaks actually work and cut down on the frustration, hopefully giving you more time to focus on family or that thing you really wanna go do. Those are the things that will mean everything in the end.

The cause of a roof leak can have a trillion different possibilities right? Wrong! As my shop teacher use to say, "Keep it simple stupid!" It can be a trillion different things if we let ourselves get carried away. We will simplify all of that with close accuracy and figure out whats really going on, and how to complete that task in a timely manner. Stick with the plan, follow the steps. If you do, you can easily identify some good candidates while eliminating all other possibilities and be pretty darn certain of your accuracy. I know this because I've done it every day for many years the hard way, then learned how to do it the right way. It came with many sleepless nights. Not having any real training is as stressful as being a surgeon with no training what so ever and being ordered to operate on a family members brain. Its a hard life already without adding more stress, and we don't want to take that stress and frustration home with us or transfer those emotions to other customers and our loved ones. Let's reduce it for us all. Especially for you!

Sometimes, the most simple roof repairs on a commercial/ industrial roof are almost impossible to solve at times. In all cases its usually due to unusual circumstances. That is what this book addresses. Warning: it does take basic math and some thinking and for some reason you may run into a lot of prime numbers. Again don't worry, were going to build a scale in your brain. Its already there, you don't know how to use it yet. You don't need to understand the numbers more than the meaning behind them. The numbers tell us things. The numbers can tell us whats been going on within the system. Remember, R.S.I. As a repair person, that shouldn't be too difficult for you. Everything written about in this book is about the detail. When making repairs, anywhere, always pay attention to the detail.

Another thing, there are no 10 roofers or repairmen that have failed or screwed up more than myself. If you read and utilize this book and run into a failure some where along the way, don't worry about it because that's how we learn. I have intentionally screwed things up to see what would happen just so I could understand what was happening, better. Everybody knew this because I like to experiment. I had to see a particular application fail to be satisfied that I knew what was going on. Guess what? I found that what people told that would happen actually didn't. Or it did happen but not in the way they said it would. For me, that makes all the difference. while planning disasters or failures I knew that roof would either be torn out destroyed or replaced anyway. Its like watching a train wreck. You know its gonna be terrible, but yet you can't look away.

Failure is only a name/label that represents a step up and nothing more, that gets us closer to success in my experience, my advice to you, plan a good failure and learn something from it, because failure will point oppositely to success.

This field guide is a culmination of many of those failures and successes. It took me about 20 years to find these solutions, and I have been increasing understanding since. I greatly hope this information helps you as much as it has helped me. For all you roof repairmen and women out there that do the hard job every day, the job that keeps the operating rooms operating, the police stations problem free, the electrical companies from having complete meltdowns or the crypts of our loved ones dry, I salute you. You do a hard thing, every day, thank you. (During the completion of this book J. L. Foster suffered a traumatic brain injury, this will probably be his last contribution to the field.)

This book is dedicated to Lisa, Christian and Alexis, I love you more than the earth and stars.

Contents

Chapter 1

Introduction

   Thank you for reading The Commercial and Industrial Roof Repair Field Guide: Strategies Theories and Proper Search Techniques. That have been written to give very blanketed oversight as to how to identify, track and locate specific roof related/non roof related problems so the proper repair can be made by the repair personnel(s) own discretion quickly and efficiently by following a common process of elimination during active investigation.

Easy simple roof leak calls are typically not hard to find, unless someone was up against commercial and industrial roof leaks that are extremely difficult due to vast or wide spaces, circumstances. Even diagnosing unusual commonalities can become a huge nuisance, unless you have dealt with these types of scenarios you probably would not understand or appreciate this information. This book expresses and explores these theories with EPDM in mind/mostly however, these theories are the same for all types of flat and commercial roofs in general.

We will discuss common roof repair search and find processes and their basic follow through structures. Most important of all, we will go over what is expected and what can be achieved with the proper tools and training. When searching out any roof related item you will always follow the same steps as to confirm or to disprove a commonality, an element or identifier/indicator, etc,. Do take into consideration that different types of roofing material made from different elements affect how a roof leak behaves.

Finding the entry point where the water is getting in from, can be and usually is, the most difficult and expensive part of the task. This guide will help you eliminate negative processes, while cutting down on work and worry so that you can concentrate on doing the highest quality job possible, with the least amount of restraints and time. Smooth running jobs are always the best jobs.

Many most likely have not heard the words, Trough Search or Perpendicular and Parallel Strategies, Internal Thermal Identification on the roof top before, so be prepared for some learning. Don't worry, this book is written by a roof repair specialist, for roof repairmen who want to specialize in advanced search techniques and strategies. This is expressed in our language.

We all need a certain amount of training, no matter what we are doing. This is especially true for actually locating a roof related problem with a high degree of success. Understanding how items that make up a roof work together such as material, or even basic construction and installation, is a big plus that will only aid in all of your investigations. Watching how buildings are built and participating in this is an even yet a bigger help.

If you do understand construction, you're ahead of the game. It's not necessary to be in the construction trade to understand how a basic roof leak works, but it does help to know a little something about basic building materials, especially absorption rates.

Some roof leaks can create emergency situations, which may affect the customer in a very negative manner. We could be in a situation where we may have to keep productive places producing by deactivating a roof leak, and if we can't the customer will get some one else who can in a big hurry.

Surprising to some is, that all roof leaks or roof related problems leave some type of evidence, even an eyewitness to the activity, is evidence. This evidence if collected, documented and utilized properly, will lead us to a solid solution within a reasonable amount of time. Therefore, if we utilize the information properly, we will not have to worry about other contractors or roofers moving in on our customers just because of one very difficult roof related issue. Its not the 99 repairs that are made successfully that will get you in trouble, its the one very important one that keeps repeating that will get a company kicked out for good.

Ultimately, the information in this book will increase your success rate. What is a success rate? A success rate is based on how many successful roof repairs you have in relation to unsuccessful roof repairs over a period of time as measured out in a ratio. We go by tens and hundreds.

If we made ten roof repairs, and two still leaked after repairs were completed, and we had to go back, our success rate is eighty percent or 80%. This is really good, not great but really good. Eventually the number will be based on, how many were unsuccessful, out of a hundred roof leak calls. After every 100, we start over. We want a 100% success rate. When you can make 100+1 roof repairs consistently you can claim the title of Master Roof Repairman.

What's the difference between a repairman and a repair specialist? 30%! He who is called back less is the most specialized, make sense? These success rates can change dramatically due to weather conditions as well, and its not always the repair persons fault if a roof related problem cannot be solved or stopped. Average success rates for a typical repairman is thirty to fifty percent, while the average success rate for a Repair specialist is ninety five to one hundred percent.

Roof repairman
Average Success Rate 30 to 50%.

Repair specialist
Average Success Rate 95 to 100%.

*True Roof Repair Opinion Ratio**

0 to 30%	Considered:	Very Poor Average	Helper/greenhorn
30 to 50%	Considered:	Accepted Average	Median Repair man/woman
50 to 75%	Considered:	Good Average	Above Median Repair man/woman
75 to 85%	Considered:	Above Average	Established Roof Repairman/woman
85 to 95%	Considered:	Great Average	Roof Repair Specialist
95 to 100%	Considered:	Excellent	Master Roof Repairman/woman
101% to +	Considered:	Above Excellent	Master Repair Specialist

*These ratios are based on the average repair person with ten years experience or more.

Because weather and circumstances can interfere with an investigation and can actually go beyond your control, averages must reflect that fact. For instance, a person would in fact have a status of a Master Roof Repairman/woman by successfully solving 8.5% of the roof repairs made out of 9.5% of attempted roof repairs. However, a Master Repair Specialist must have 100 continuous fully solved roof repairs, plus one more to gain the status of Master Repair Specialist. Again, 101 complete and solved roof repairs must be made to claim this title. This only has to be done once to be achieved. There is also the second option. If you are a repairman/woman and average 95 to 100% success for ten years and no less, that earns the title of Master Roof Repairman/woman. Two ways to achieve this plateau and a thousand ways to loose it.

What can a Master Repair Specialist accomplish when on the roof?

Identify the maker of the material, the amount of roofs.

Must be able to identify past problems, repairs easily.

Find any new/current roof/non-roof related issues/problems.

Identify any future problems, such as loose details, penetrations or deep scrapes in the membrane, etc,.

Collect all evidence, measurements.

Utilize advanced search techniques efficiently.

Make the minimal amount of repairs while allowing for the proper flashing times so patches are proper and permanent.

That is achieved with confidence within thee hours on an average size or 50,000 square foot building with a smooth EPDM roof.

After a while you loss column will shrink more and more as the challenges seem to be smaller and simpler. Roof leaks whether related to the roof or not fall into one category or another. As they fall out of one category, they fall into another automatically.

Bottom line.

Success rate is not based on installation of penetrations. A Master Repair Specialist not only has a success rate of 100% plus success rate, or over 100 plus roof repairs at a time without a call back but, this individual is also capable of installing all types and sizes of penetrations on all types of roofs and is able to control all types of water emergencies in all types of circumstances. This must be achieved with no roof leaks.

We have been in some circumstances where the rain fell heavily and there was no stopping the water, but instead we have the ability to divert and control the problem until conditions allowed us to be more effective later. This book is not about numbers or stats more than it is about getting our customers out of troubling circumstances This success rate, your success rate will go up against nature. You will loose. That is not a failure however. Doing absolutely nothing about it, not serving your customers needs, that is the failure. Don't be surprised if your success rate is affected by weather events that go beyond your control, like working in total darkness, while in a down pour with flashlights, one must be fair to effort and simple truth?

Deep water, mud and even lightning over head, many of us have had that experience. If you are facing lightning or dangerous circumstances, get off the roof immediately. I used to stay in those dangerous situations to protect my success rate. Not worth it, the storm will pass. Have some coffee and wait somewhere safe. There are many circumstances that affect success rates, your safety trumps any and all success rates always.

Some employers do offer training for repairman, but very few in my thirty plus years of experience. For training they say, "Just find the hole and patch it." Congratulations, you have just received the same top-notch training as most of us roof repairmen and women. After learning how to apply different types of patches, you're good to go. Obviously, there is much more to it than that.

Quicker, smarter to the source is our achievable goal

More times than not, it will not be the process of elimination for the typical roof repair technician and this can be expensive, especially when you eliminate one item each trip out to the customer. We for the most part look for holes, patch things that look like a problem until the leak hopefully and thankfully goes away.

Some repairmen are luckier and some are more aware and do better. Sometimes you can have a lucky stretch and have nothing but easy roof leak calls. On the flip side, you can have a slew of terrible roof leak calls in a row that never seem to end, which might wipe out your high rate in what might seem like a flash. These stack of high risk calls with possible damage to property and possibly reputation if not found and fixed, are the part of the over all equation that we can improve on if we eliminate the negative processes that come along with them. We must eliminate repeat calls, sometimes, going back time after time cannot be avoided under the perfect storm of circumstances.

All roofs/roof leaks have commonalities. These commonalities will be connecting the leak/roof and the related problem(s) together, somehow. To less complicate things, all of these commonalities are directly tied to indicators. In essence, there can only be so many problems to find regardless, but there are positive/negative indicators that can point us to a specific problem and away from thousands of other false positives.

These examples are very generic/basic but do follow a common course that you will come across in most cases on flat, commercial or industrial roofs in general, this is a general theory and you need to understand it in order to succeed. Ballasted roofs are obviously more difficult.

Sometimes, you have to move the gravel until you find the entry point. Don't worry; there are some tips in here that may help save time on these most difficult scenario types of roofs as well.

Material such as EPDM/Built-up, heat weld, etc., does not come with a list of, this is what you may find if it starts to leak, or this is where the problem is if it starts leaking here, or over there. This is true for all types of roofing material or products. Roof leaks or any roof related problem depends on everything physically/historically associated with the roof in general, and that roof related problem can be quite unique in respect to the roof.

For too long many have essentially come up with the solution or found the cut hole, slice and/or roof related problem without really doing the math or hit and miss approach is the way of the world it seems, without being able to explain it in a universal language thats more modern and a process thats more dependable and fundamental. For the most part many technicians stumble on, or find their offending entry point by accident, with virtually no understanding of how or why. We just make the repair and hope the next one is just as easy. Then there are those who even with a compass, laser and a roof repair finding eye dog (all you have to do is train one with the smell of different types of rotting insulation) still can never find the actual problem.

Matter of fact, there are repair people who have made a career out of going back time after time on the same roof leak, and never was fired for not finding the problem. Why was that? Because no one else could do any better with that particular roof repair, thats why. One guy did find it eventually, and I kept that contract for many years, until I retired.

This is of utmost importance too, getting a good helper. If your helper is not interested in the adventure of searching out a mystery with very few clues, get rid of that person. Fact of the matter is, a typical repair person has a fifty-fifty chance of finding any given roof leak/roof related problem on any given day, just like everyone else in the world would be allowed.

Those odds are for the good repair tech. That success rate increases drastically when your helper knows what he or she is suppose to be doing. Having a good helper or assistant makes all the difference, this is vitally important choose wisely.

Some repair foremen sit around while they work their helpers to death. Don't do that. He or she is there to assist, not to do it all! It is an unwritten law for repair people, a foreman and helper share the work equally. There is brain work, but more than anything else, there will be physical labor. All of these processes and procedures are equal in thinking and physical labor. Share them equally when ever possible.

One of the biggest rules for many repairmen is, if any one ever needs help on the roof, help them. This also includes your helper. Some of us have been on the roof as a helper while the foreman was busy with non-roof related issues. Then when enough work wasn't done in the eight-hour day, they would blame the helper for not working hard enough. That is one reason why there are fights in the roof repair business. Advanced search techniques must include work from both equally. First, let's look at what a good helper does.

What good helpers do

A good helper will

Show up on time, dressed for work and prepared for anything from a simple repair, to going out of state for a few days on an emergency call <u>everyday</u>.

Check the oil, fluids of the work vehicles, keep your vehicle clean, and fully stocked with all materials every morning, and at least enough to complete an entire array of patches for every single type of roof you maybe working on, and more than enough material to do so.

Clean the living space of your vehicle, make sure everything under the seats belongs there. Remove all trash and wipe down interior especially during long trips.

Keep track of written information such as gas mileage, hours worked and drawings or maps, and to store this information so it is easily retrieved.

Work the same hours as the foremen and work as hard as the foreman. Sometimes over a hundred patches may need to be applied during one repair call, that's fifty patches apiece. Share the wealth!

A good helper has to have a good personality, and not look threatening. A good helper always falls back from the foreman and or supervisor and customer when they are discussing the work load, and is always respectful.

A good helper is always aware of safety requirements. A ten-hour training card from OSHA for helpers and foremen at a minimum is well recommended. Repairmen and helpers often go beyond the usual spectrum of typical roof related hazards and additional safety training maybe required in relation to your many work environments.

A good helper will have a valid driver's license and be capable of driving a variety of vehicles. This includes forklifts, high-lifts and manual transmission vehicles. Having a drivers license is not necessary to get or keep a job as a helper as a drivers license is not required to drive on private property. If they don't know how to operate these other types of vehicles, but they worth the effort take the time to show them how to operate all machinery safely. It really does pay off in the long run for everyone.

When the foreman needs a break from driving or materials need to be retrieved and the only extra body is the helper, it makes a big difference. If you have a helper who is working out well, keep that person whether they have license or not. Good helpers aren't easy to find. If you do find a good helper that has a valid drivers license, the over all capability of your crew increases.

Often a roofing company or foreman will have a program or arrange for a helper to receive his drivers license.

It's a great feeling to be successful when solving the unsolvable. It definitely would not have been that easy for myself without a good helper. Make sure you share the credit with the helper, and you the supervisor takes all the blame. Its your job, your responsible for yourself and your crew no matter how small or large. You always get all the blame for everything that goes wrong. Sorry, job requirement. This is where it gets real.

Historically helpers are not paid well, usually a little better pay than a laborer. It's asking a lot of a person to work this hard, and under difficult weather conditions for such a low rate. Some helpers will put aside the money issue in hopes of becoming a repair foreman someday. This essential sacrifice makes the roofing world go around. If a helper pays attention and understands the process, they too can become a repairman or even a repair specialist. Who knows, you might be working for him or her some day.

One of the most important and difficult aspects of your job you may have noticed is the paper work. It is the helper/assistant's job to keep track of these paper items after, you have received them. You probably collect gas receipts, or maybe its electronic receipts most of the time, but either way, you will collect receipts along your travels. Most of us have systems to handle and understand what can be a massive amount of paperwork in a six day week.

Some weeks, just a couple of receipts which is easy to keep up with, some weeks its inches of thick paper work and hopefully the days won't over lap. Containers and short or midget file cabinets have worked fine for myself. Often in the center of the back wall of the work truck/van has always been ample room for home made shelves and or small file cabinets or container holders of all types.

Plastic containers are excellent for keeping receipts dry and in good order. Often, despite all of this work to keep everything in order, every now and then we would still loose a receipt. This is caused by simply not putting the receipt away in the appropriate dry, clean location so it may be quickly collected when all paperwork is due. For many of us its on monday morning when all the paperwork must be turned in and it must be complete.

Sometimes the accounting people will let you slide, but they have to write checks and if they don't have your hours or your employees hours, they can't pay you, or your crew. Of course you know the quickest way to make some one pretty upset is not having a pay check on pay day. Almost everyone who has been involved in roofing in one form or another has gone through this. Its a real tough thing to go through a whole week especially when you counted on the money being there, then suddenly its not.

Its strongly recommended that you organize. Spend two or three hours of your own time to organize your office space and do this once a month if possible. Of course the office space is the cab of your work truck or van. Make sure your work space/office is clean. Nothing screams professional more than a clean work vehicle. Its the first thing customers see when you arrive and the last thing they see when you leave the premises.

There is a big difference between cluttered and dirty. Most of us who make a living on the road take stuff with us from home and we can collect a lot of it. As cool and sentimental as they are, these small items can become projectiles during an accident and you should avoid having them laying around especially on the dash board. If your a dad or mom you will probably collect a lot of home made stuff from your kids and its good to have these priceless heirlooms. Again, containers. Keep them clean and safe and they will not become a projectile during a life changing accident.

Do not go beyond your limits when it comes to driving long distances for long periods of time. This is a very serious safety issue. We very much want to get back home to make schedules and appointments, please slow down. Its easy to get overwhelmed with too many things on our plate. The most important thing to do is not to get excited. Taking your time and thinking through your task seems like a waste of time for some people because they feel the can do without safety or some organization. Take the time to be safe and keep well organized with completed paper work that is ready to be turned in on time.

Unfortunately, we often complete our paperwork at home. All paper work is to be completed on the job site, with the times, dates and signatures, and with pictures if required. If you stay with this scheduling, you can stay on top of the paperwork and avoid doing any paperwork at home. This brings down the stress level a thousand percent, highly recommended.

Makes notes for these papers, keep a stapler in your office and staple the notes to the receipts or paperwork. Yes, staplers can be written off your taxes. As long as it is being utilized for your work, its deductible or part is, check with your tax rep to be sure.

A lot of repairmen/women don't realize and many roofers for that part is that everything you wear and your office expenses can be written off your taxes. Old school roofers got the best equipment and work related clothing, it was a write off and thats why the got the best and coolest things, our uncle same ultimately paid for them. You do not have to get the best of the best, do spend your money for what works for you. Take good care of your tools, work clothes and by all means keep your receipts. Again, have a container for your write off work related equipment and clothing account, and keep this container in your home close to your tax papers.

Residuals from chapter 1

This book covers the theories and applications processes and strategies for identifying and locating while differentiating between roof/non-roof related problems effectively and efficiently.

These theories and applications, processes are typical for all types of flat roofs, this book specifies E.P.D.M.

Read this field guide at home first, and then take it on the roof.

Keep track of your success rate.

Success rate of Green horn is 30% or less.

Success rate of Repair Specialist is 95 to 100%.

Success rate for a Master Roof Repair Specialist is 101%.

Get and keep a good helper.

Treat your helper with respect.

Share all physical labor and credit with your helper 50/50.

Repairmen/foremen and Specialist take blame for all mistakes his or her crew causes.

Keep you office/work space clean and functional.

Make sure all paper work is completed at the end of each job.

Make sure you and your helper are keeping track of all receipts and paperwork.

Turn all paperwork in on time and with all signatures and photos.

Keep all work related receipts for tax purposes (Work boots/clothing, paper clips, etc,.

Chapter 2

Public Relations and Preparation

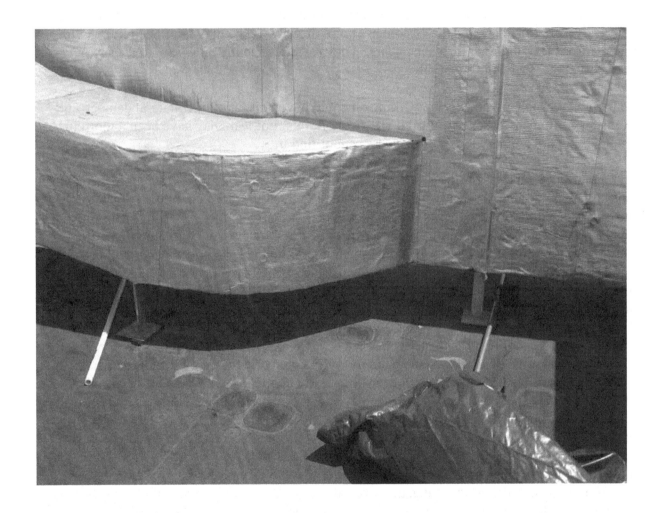

It can be very difficult to define what makes a customer happy, since all customers are different. First, the leak/roof related problem must be stopped. Removing the unwanted activity is only part of the bigger picture when serving a customers needs.

When it rains I say, "Here that?, Pennies from heaven!" There would not be any pennies from heaven if the customer did not believe in my ability to make the proper repair in a professional manner, or if the customer did not like me on some level. In addition, it is true, if the customer does not like you on a personal level, it would not matter how many leaks were stopped, and they would most likely request someone else to serve their roof related needs.

In some cases, a customer may choose someone who may not be as effective, but the customer likes that repair tech enough to allow breathing room. You cannot always make friends with the customer but having a professional persona is a good solid place to start. It is always our customer's choice who serves their roof top needs, not yours.

We want that choice to be a good one, every time our customers do business with us

Before you go out to meet the customer consider a positive and constructive approach if you do not already. Try to understand the customer's point of view. They may have been living with a particular roof leak for a while, maybe years. They might be feeling, how should we say, "A little upset about the whole situation."

The particular problem you may be working on could have done a lot of collateral damage and the customer, in many cases has heard it all. In short, this roof leak may have been a thorn in their side and you are only the next one, who cannot find it.

Something super important is the way you look. Be sure crew appearance is at least acceptable. Honestly, no one wants to see a two tooth, hair unwashed, clothes torn up, broken down truck, kind of a person telling them they fixed the problem after being up there on the roof for only 10 minutes! Try to act, and look professional. Do not be arrogant or over confident, those are things real professionals never do. A professional impression goes a long way with all customers despite failure or their personal view of you. After all you are human, you will fail, lets do it in a professional way. But professionals really don't fail, they find another path around the problem, that's the secret road to success.

A weakness in the roof repair industry is that we have no way of monitoring effective roof repair people and their strategies, because there are no well known or understood strategies that can be tested or proven to date. Should the roof repair industry be monitored? Monitoring would weed out the bad apples and most likely add to the pay scale for the good ones. Besides, the rip-off artists do a lot of damage to the roof repair industry, and the legitimate roof repair person pays the price. They do the crime and we do the time. There should be a database somewhere.

Of all the trades, roofing and or roof repair people wages have come down, over time that is. Other professional trades have testing, accountability and specialized training that justifies their pay scale. Due to the long-term costs increases, when the construction industry suffers from recession, the larger paid trade scales are the first to suffer. This has made roofing/repair work in general, almost recession proof, but low paying. Somehow we should find a middle ground with accounted testing and new training that justify the pay scale. That will be left to the Office of Roof Repair Accountability. That doesn't exist, yet.

Over all you will have outstanding customer relationships if you solve their problem or make their roof stop leaking in one trip, and in a professional way. If you do not solve the problem, they can be very difficult and sometimes mean. Do not take it personally its only business.

There are some customers who are very emotional, and take everything you do and say to heart, or twist the story around just to cause trouble. Be careful of what you speak of and what you speak about. Some people may be having a bad day and then YOU show up. Nothing political, religious or supernatural should ever be brought into a conversation with a customer. They are allowed their opinion; just let them have their say. Keep your personal opinions to yourself. Do not take it personally again, its only business.

Sometimes no matter how hard or intense repairmen work to solve a roof leak it wont stop, it can and will make a full circle throughout the roofing community, and come back again to you, or to your company. It is some what strange, but that is how it works more often than not. If this does happen which it might, we may be face to face with a customer that got pissed off, the first time around. Fortunately, for your customer, you will be armed with the most extensive amount of information on the subject of roof related problems/roof leaks that exists hopefully since that visit.

Always follow all safety requirements from OSHA. Some corporations, companies, or even yourself, may have safety requirements that exceed OSHA standards. As the most important rule of all, OSHA standards must always be obeyed at the very minimum. When all is said and done, OSHA is protecting you and your life, always bet on that.

Special thanks to OSHA, we know that they have saved our lives more than once over the years thanks to safe practices. Back in the day, people went and did that very dangerous job, and if they did not, those people had to go find another job. Surprised more repair people were not killed back then, because we took big risks for a dollar.

To make matters worst you had to make that decision to risk your life for a roof repair on the spot, and several repairmen have suffer severe injuries and deaths because of it. Not to mention, families of those poor souls did without fathers, husbands and sons. With your help, those numbers can go down to zero accidents and/or deaths every year, again always use all OSHA rules as a minimum standard on all roof leak calls and is always strongly recommended.

After a while, it seemed like just about every building had a roof leak that would never completely go away, kind of like an unwanted family member, that was my specialty. Never seem to get any easy leak calls. Would always get the customers who had roof leaks since they had been in business or since the building had been built. In some cases, they would have roof leaks that were permanent fixtures

In my own statistics the ratio of new leaks caused by wind damage or human traffic were small compared to the many roof related problems that appeared to be caused within the first 6 months of installation, but became active months or years later. And these same aggravating repeat types of roof related problems that were impossible to find type by other repairmen. Learned early, more training was needed because I can't fix them all.

You could also be working behind people who were careful and thoughtful of that brand new roof that was installed, and had nothing to do with the damage from a visiting contractor, who did not mention there was some accidental damage done, as he sneaked out. Visitors on the roof can cause major problems, does not matter whom, what or when. Never blame anyone for any damage, as this may come back to haunt you in a legal way. Unless you personally see the damage being done and took pictures, there is never any opinion about who caused it, period!

Make direct eye contact, do not interrupt the customer when he or she is speaking, and listen closely to what they have to say. Some customers vent loudly and others will give you un-professional treatment. At one large corporation, my two-man crew was accused of not stopping a roof leak even though we knew we had. They were not aware of it at the time, when we came back; it was for a new roof leak.

They were pleasantly surprised when they found out that we were stopping the roof leaks all over their plant. They were so use to have the same leak re-activate, they just assumed we missed it when someone made another call to our company. After stopping all the leaks, they wanted us on a big project, maintenance and future repair work. 85% of my work has been from repeat customers. We did not get mad about the false accusation either. Keep your cool, the most important thing to do in the whole world, is not to get excited or angry, about anything.

That's the good believe it or not, but what about the bad? If the fault is your own, man up and apologize your ass off. Believe me, they'll get over it. Denying it and lying about it can ruin your status and reputation in the world of roofing. More important, once the customer looses faith in you, then you and your company are finished.

Put yourself in the mindset that you will find and fix that roof leak/roof-related problem, and let the customer know you are on their side. Listen to everything the customer is saying even if they are mad as hell at you and yelling. That's called a verbal whooping. Yes, this too is only business, and you will get over it.

Learn the Jargon

Understanding the Jargon/Language is key to this book. For instance, a roof leak is not a roof leak until its proven it came through the actual roof. Many things can leak from the ceiling level, but only an entry point causes a roof leak. Matter of fact, a cut, slice, hole in the membrane of any kind is an entry point. On the other hand your entry point may be related to Other sources. Whether you have a one-inch slice on the roof or a 20 by 40 foot rip in the membrane, it is an entry point. Were not looking for leaks, were looking roof related problems, which include roof leaks. Or better yet, any way water can enter the roof or its attachments.

After you zero in on a complete and absolute problem, only then can you name it for what it is. It may be a roof leak, or a non-roof related problem/item. That is why we utilize the general descriptions. This prevents us from looking not so informed later.

What questions should you ask and how to ask them can be confusing depending on the type of personality of the customer. Try to ask the same question in a different way if you do not understand the customer the first time around. To increase your understanding of the problem, you must get as much information as possible about the activity, building/structure and past roof and non-roof related problems.

Talk to your customer as an equal. No matter how much money they do or do not have, treat them like family. I have had incredible relationships with workers, corporate presidents of some very large companies and corporations. From the janitor to the CEO, I have made wonderful friends because of respect and understanding and relentless efforts that have stopped countless roof leaks.

Not sure but after a while, we would always talk about everything else first, and lastly we would talk about the roof related problem. You can have great relationships with the customer that may become more important than the relationship with your employer. In other words, the owner of the property may not want to talk to your boss, they may want to talk to you, because you have the answers and they trust you.

In the real world, your employer may not want you to talk to your customer about specifics until you talk to them first. Always check in with your employer before approaching a customer about major issues with their roof. There may be information that your company may want to discuss with you first.

Never bring volatile materials, liquids into any business or building. Some people are hypersensitive to volatile chemicals. This is most definitely true if someone in the building may be suffering from a medical disorder.

Always pull these materials up the side or rear of the building when ever possible. If you are forced to carry in chemicals, make sure lids are closed tight and placed in a plastic bag and tied to minimize the accidental escaping of fumes.

How are you today?

How are you today is by far the most important question you can ask another person. Everyone automatically feels a higher sense of worth when someone asks him or her, how they are feeling. If no one cares, life can seem a little pointless. Yes, we care about our customer, at least enough to ask. That is why we get out of bed, just for them. This is how we show them that someone does care, we ask them. This does go a long way for most people.

Do not expect the customer to respond in a positive way to you every time. Matter of fact many customers will be met for the most part, in a time of heated battle.

For instance, you may go to a manufacturing facility, the plant manager is having disagreements with the unions, upper management, and a huge roof leak has shut down production lines. He or she may not have 10 minutes to spend with you simply because they are having a bad and busy ass day.

They will get down to business when they are ready, so be patient and respectful if they have a lot going on, or not. If they tell you to hang loose that is fine, they are paying you to sit. Do what they say. Do not go out on your own. There maybe something very important that you may need to know. Besides, no one wants someone who does not follow orders working for them, would you?

Here are some questions to ask in a more professional manner/way, and how not to ask them.

Hello, how are you today?
What up? Hello Beautiful! Sup Dude!

Our company received a call from your company regarding a roof related problem, who can we talk to about that?
You got a leak?

Is someone available to show us the location of this roof related problem?
Where's it leak'n at?

Today only, or has this particular item been active before?
Did it leak here before?

What type of rain event activates this particular problem, heavy or light rain, does anyone here have that information?
Does it have to rain hard before it starts leaking? Does it leak a lot? Any of you know?

Do you have any type of plumbing, sprinkler systems or HVAC units that may be closely associated with the problem area that you are aware of?
Is your units or plumb'n leak'n ?

Does this roof related problem/issue become active at the beginning of a rain event or later on?
Did it start leaking when it first started raining?

Do you have any roof related problems or items nearby at any other locations?
Got any other leaks?

Has there been any new construction on the roof or HVAC work lately?
Anyone been working up there?

What type of roof system do you have?
What kind of roof you got?

Where is the location of your roof access?
You got a roof hatch?

Further words and expressions are at the end of this chapter

Get the point? You can project real professionalism that truly makes all the difference just in the way you choose your words. If successful with your search, and you find a solution to the problem on the first trip, this usually adds up to a customer for life.

These are general suggestions; you have to admit roof related problem sounds more professional than roof leak. How would you want a professional to speak to you? You expect a professional for your service needs; you must afford the same to your customers. There is never an exception to this rule if professionalism is your goal.

Some roof leaks come and go it seems seasonally or intermittently. This really does happen due to weather and physics. All roofs have a direct connection to weather and in the end, it will boil down to three things, time, rate, and amount. Even though some roof related problems will only become active during a ten year rain event, other pesky leaks become active when the winds blows the rain a certain direction. Where and when and how much, is important information to you.

Most legitimate roof leaks become active at every rain event, while HVAC unit leaks are often subjected to heavy humidity and clogged J-Trap situations. Other items that also cause non-roof related leaks would be walls or windows that may also face a certain direction. These are some of the reasons why the customer's information is so very important, it may tell us where to begin the search, and where to take it to in a quicker manner. You might to be surprised where you end up. That's the fun part!

Some roofs can take in water through the system, but not actively leak. For instance, some roof related problems that do not become active during a rain event, but only after the event is over. In some rare cases, less than 4% of some roof related problems will persist and leak on for days afterwards, but not a drop during the rain event. This is just the nature of the beast. This is what

17

we are going to learn about, how to identify, discuss, calculate and solve from as many aspects as possible.

Despite everything you read and see here, do not be surprised if you find unique items during your searches out in the field. Everyone is counting on you to expand this information more, long after our time is over. It is very likely that some may run into something no one has ever seen before, hopefully its you.

E or E ratio, what does that mean? Entry point, exit point. Some place on the roof there is a place where the water is getting in at. That may be a cut, hole or slice, who knows what it could be. Below in the business we have a leak. Where the entry point is and where the exit point is will be a ratio based on distance. The smaller the ratio, the easier the repair, the simpler the search the quicker the repair.

Ignored on purpose is what some do

Some customers ignore certain roof leaks on purpose. They have just simply spent enough time and money on it, and they are finished with it. We may not even be allowed to talk about it anymore, you don't know. That bucket may come out and be placed under the roof leak for years and years every time it rains. Surprisingly, it is okay to the customer.

It is not unusual to occasionally see, an entire drop ceiling littered with multiple buckets/pans hidden away on top of the ceiling tracking and pads. It is primarily a safety issue and should not be allowed. Water weights about 8 pounds per gallon. Do not let your customer ignore a roof leak. If a customer has gone to the point of ignoring a roof leak, then all hope is lost. Your job is to give them back that hope.

Some of these ignored roof leaks may not be reported because they do not bother anyone, or anything of importance. Nevertheless, if the customer has other roof related problems near by the area you are investigating, that old problem could lead to the causes and solutions to the new problem that the customer called about.

Never leave a roof leak behind. Believe you me, we have had to leave a location with more leaks to find, but we had to pull away to go to a bigger disaster where there was a danger of explosion, because of water dripping on an electrical panel. The first place I went to after the big disaster was the business that I had to pull away from, that will be the only reason you leave behind an active roof related problem.

Before we left the major problem to go to a bigger major problem, we hung up plastic with tape and diverted the water into a small barrel to put the leak in a state of control, until we could return. Always take control of the activity one way or another.

Always look for old staining and ceiling tile damage, even though there are no active roof leaks in those areas. That information can show us what happened in the past. Many businesses however often change out their ceiling tiles, always ask if they have.

Ask everyone the questions that you asked the original contact. You will be surprised how certain people know more than others. A plumbing problem or maybe something unreported may only needed pointing out by the only person that knows about it.

Get this information and any other requests you might have. Common needs such as parking, restrooms and water fountains. Most roof repair people and women often do not have good access to restrooms and water fountains. Were often treated like homeless criminals. To access these areas we should always have clean boots/shoes or disposable slippers. Otherwise, you might have to pay large carpet cleaning bills. This creates a negative experience for the customer and a black eye for you and your company.

Try to prepare, don't do things like accidentally take cell phones into restricted areas. Each time your company or crew get involved in any type of negative incident, your company has a mark against it in the eyes of the customer. A positive experience every time will make all the difference in the long run.

Make sure you have stepladders, flashlights, and brooms, shovels and trash bags in case you make a mess. You never know what to expect so always have P.P.E. equipment as well. We will go over all this later.

When making a permanent roof repair always use the same brand name of material that is on that particular flat roof. Although most materials are almost identical, some unique attributes make the material different from each manufacturer respectively.

Utilizing compatible brands of material is recommended over all. No matter the brand of material, that particular material was designed to work with itself. Different brands of material expand and contract at different rates, and there will always be a contradiction in the form of uneven action per layer, that will eventually cause an additional problem or patch failure in the future. Might take a while, but it will happen.

Keep customers in the loop at every turn in your investigation whether its good or bad news, immediately let them know what's happening either minor or major, after checking in with your employer. Always check in and never leave a job site without checking out with your customer. Its poor predicate to mysteriously disappear without any explanation. It is just as bad to suddenly show up and be working without signing in or checking in with someone on site. This lack of information can lead to fatalities. If you do not sign in with the customer and they do not know you or your crew is there, emergency workers will not be looking for you if there is a fire or dangerous situation. Why would they, technically your not there.

What should you take inside when first investigating a roof leak? What could you possibly need? Once inside after meeting with the customer it does not look good to be heading out to your truck getting one thing after another.

The old school roofers would kick you for having to make more than one trip for anything. In them days, you carried something up the ladder and OSHA could not say anything about it. Thankfully that has changed. Were prepared, but in a safe way.

Essential tools for a Repair Specialist

Digital Camera
Small hand level
Compass
Step ladder
Marble or ball barring
Small notebook, pencil/pen
Laser Pointer
High powered mini flashlight
Probe
Multi-tip screw driver
Stop watch of some type
Glass or plastic measuring container
Trash bags/hand brush/mini broom
Thermometer, Manual or Digital
Stethoscope
Measuring Wheel

A book bag holds everything pretty well and additional compartments can be added in to hold everything in its place, so it can be transferred from ground to roof seamlessly.

Hang up as much material and tools as you can on the walls of your work vehicle, to eliminate layers and layers of crap you have to dig through, when it should only take a couple of minutes, not twenty. Do not charge the customer for disorganization.

You cannot avoid these tools, they make finding a roof leak more certain by giving you real information that you absolutely do need. Try to collect as many of these as you can until you have them all. For the most part, they are not that expensive and easy to use.

A good probe is similar to a welding rod or a thin piece of metal or plastic. Length approximately 7 inches and somewhat flexible. Thickness should be no less than an eighth of an inch, no more than a quarter of an in diameter with rounded ends. Probes are what we utilize to test for openings at laps and possible entry points. Keep it in your pocket, as you will be using it a lot.

Proper predicate continued

Roof leak = Roof related problem

Penetration leak/pipe leak = Non roof related problem

Light/heavy rain, thunderstorms/drizzle = Rain Event

Patch = Repair

Roof access = Roof hatch

Specialized tools = All the tools in your book bag

Roof = Roof system

Residuals from Chapter 2

Always check in with the customer.

Be respectful and professional to all, especially to helpers.

Never disrupt a place of business, block or obstruct walkways/work at any place of production or service during a roof leak call for any reason unless it is to save a life or property.

Arrive prepared (tools, materials and attitude).

Wear disposable slippers (Shoe covers) when inside any business.

Never take volatile chemicals into the customers work place unless necessary.

<u>Listen to the customer</u> and understand their unique specific needs and roof related problems.

Follow the customer's directions.

Speak in a professional manner.

Keep personal opinions to ones self.

Collect information associated with the leak location and its history.

Report information to your boss, then to your customer.

Always utilize the same brand material in relation to the roof you are working on.

If a repair cannot be made, divert the water with plastic sheeting into a vessel or bucket.

Always clean up any mess, your crew makes.

It is not a crime to help a customer clean up a mess directly caused by a roof related problem when the scale of the debris or required complete clean up may only take a few minutes of your time.

Always check out with the customer and that there are no other questions the customer has that you can answer.

Complete all paperwork before going to the next customer and collect signatures if needed.

Chapter 3

Anatomy of a Roof Leak

    Why does a roof leak behave the way it does and what are the components of a legitimate roof leak? Luckily, for everyone involved a legitimate roof leak can be identified, confirmed or debunked by five main factors. These factors will always be negative or positive. We want to be absolutely sure based on the facts on hand that what were are witnessing is exactly what we are seeing, even though its not very clear. These major to minor hints/indicators or even commonalities depending on your point of view help us in the long run.

There are many possible causes that mimic a roof leak, we need to be sure from the beginning what we are looking at is truly a roof leak, after all we don't want to be mislead from the beginning of our investigation or confused along the way.

These five factors/indicators make the activity much easier to understand and track down. After all, it is very difficult to imagine or understand what happens when water enters into a roof system and finally exits out somewhere random when you cannot see between the layers of what makes up a roof or layers of roof. These indicators will narrow down possible causes and affects and help direct you in a big way.

Most roofs have an incipient amount of deficiencies that could be the source of many different types of roof related problems. Problem is 99% of those deficiencies will have nothing to do with the roof related problem that you may be looking for. We can walk around all day long pointing out things that don't look exactly right or maybe not up to par, but not be the cause of the offending issue. Just because something looks poor cosmetically does not mean it is the cause of a roof leak. Matter of fact we will no longer specify roof leak. It is now a roof related problem until properly labeled one way or another.

As mentioned earlier, without X-Ray vision we cannot see between the decking and the roof membrane however, no matter what type of roof it is, these indicators make the roof related problem a legitimate roof leak instead of a vent leak/non-roof related item or forever unknown. There are things we can do and things to look for that will give us definite answers. Approaching all problems pragmatically and practically is the structured basis for these theories.

One simple indicator can eliminate a leak call by simply witnessing and photographing water draining from a leaking sprinkler system. On the other hand, that same person can make a mistake, not paying attention and miss a roof leak running along side of the sprinkler leak. One can be prematurely chased away by the fact that it may not be roof related, but a Repair Specialist will not only confirm the leak is actively draining from a pipe, but he or she will also inspect the roof and find that roof leak running tandem with the sprinkler pipe leak. A Specialist wouldn't walk away with a dual roof and non-roof related problem going on at the same location without investigating completely, would they?

This is where going the extra mile pays off. Everything in this book is going the extra mile in every aspect.

These of course are common sense steps. These indicators that go along with what is the deciding factor of what is a genuine roof leak is what can save you time by knowing where your suppose to be looking. If you know what you are up against you then know how to plan and execute your next steps efficiently. Every day is different, like every leak call is different. Knowing if it is a actual roof leak right away will decide on whether you are; doing your job, know what your doing, whether you are paying attention, wasting someone else's money, or are an actual repair person or repair specialist or a wanna be. This can be decided on just one job, and this reputation can stick with you for your entire life. We usually don't pick which job will haunt us for the rest of our lives. Sometimes a person can do one thing only one time and be labeled with that for the rest of their lives and this is true for certain jobs.

24

If your not looking for these factors/indicators and decided on whether they are positive or negative or not, you are probably making mistakes along the way. These mistakes if made at the very beginning of your investigation can greatly hamper your search from start to finish. You may spend large amounts of your customers money and net nothing but negative results. No one would want a visiting roofer to accidentally find that you missed, even if it was just a small opening along a metal flashing that activated a non-roof related leak that you over looked by accident and it should have been noticed easily.

First we will briefly go over the fundamentals in this chapter of the anatomy of a roof leak and the following chapters will cover each more in depth. Even though all roof leaks are different they are also basically the same in make up and how they work mechanically. Roof leaks act and do very specific things.

Anatomy of a Roof Leak

Two types of roof leaks over all, developed or sudden

ELIMINATION OF OTHER SOURCES

EXIT POINTS

PATH OF TRAVEL

RESERVOIRS

ENTRY POINTS

ELIMINATION OF OTHER SOURCES

The elimination of other sources that feed a suspected roof leak is paramount in solving any roof related problem/item. Eliminating other sources will always be the first step in any and all roof and non-roof leak related investigations.

EXIT POINTS

Exit points can be only one drip/leak, multiple drips or pouring water draining from a roof related problem/item or non-roof related problem/item. When you have more than handful of exit points/leaks scattered around a relatively small area that 's classified as Spider webbing.

PATH OF TRAVEL

There are three paths of travel. One directly tied to decking that follows channels or the flutes of the deck itself. The second path will be through/around over and under insulation. The third applies to non-roof related items such as units/penetrations.

RESERVOIRS

Reservoirs also known as water filled channels of decking or bladders of water within the system. Reservoirs can exist through out the roof and lay just about any where water can collect and build up.

ENTRY POINTS

Entry points cover all openings that allow water into the building. This includes cuts in the membrane, slices and tears. Also, this includes openings around HVAC units flashings. Whether these be roof related or not an entry point allows water directly into the building.

POSITIVE OR NEGATIVE

Determining whether an item is negative or positive is an extremely important exercise.

Variables

Variables are the unknowns. Things that change such as measurements or weights. Lengths and distances are also variables that you should be paying attention to. These variables although they may change per individual roof, they may keep a common number or scenario. Let us look at a quick example of a variable related to a reservoir. The variable for that reservoir is how much water is lying in the bottom of the deck, or how much water is part of that reservoir? The variable would be the best guess amount in the channel of the decking.

An entry point through the roof membrane is to a positive indicator, the variable is how big the entry point is. An exit point is a positive indicator and the variable would be how much water is dripping out of that exit point. Variables are covered more in depth from different angles, as all of this information is connected together to one body.

You will see two types of roof leaks over all. We have developed or sudden. Of course if you poke a hole in a roof in a low lying area there is a good chance it may leak relatively quick during the first rain event, but development of a roof leak can take years before becoming visible or active. Another new word you will use a lot is, "active, "Active means someone witnessed water actually dripping from an exit point right now," in real time. Non-active means it's not active now, but it was at some time, it is that simple.

We have found evidence that an entry point was accidentally made at a particular time, and we measured and estimated the time as to when it was made, and when it became active. Was somewhat amazed at first, I always thought that when a hole was made on the roof it would leak immediately or at the first rain event. Not true in many cases. Most roof related items investigated on average will have a head start. Sudden roof leaks are just that, sudden. Sudden roof leaks are usually easy to find compared to long term developed roof leaks.

Sometimes, something happens on the roof, like a contractor's carelessness or something blew across the roof and made an entry point or several. Springing up from nowhere, these sudden type roof related problems usually leak hard and fast in a typical rain event. A sharp item can penetrate the roof, cutting through the membrane, then the insulation and hit the deck. This will funnel an instant and large leak out of what seems, all of a sudden.

What do we do when we see an active roof leak dripping from the ceiling? What do you do? Touching the dripping water is something I cannot keep from. This simple touch has told me a lot about the source. For instance if the water is hot, then we know it may be produced by something like, a water heater or steam pipe. If the water is cold to the touch, or colder than the outside conditions are, then we know it could be an HVAC problem. If the water temperature is outside temperature then it could be a legitimate roof leak, in most cases. Do not forget to wash your hands after touching any fluids from any job site. This is where the thermometer comes into use. A thermometer can confirm these suspicions.

An active leak is so valuable. Some see leaking and say, "Oh No! I say, "Cool, some direction." This activity can tell us so much about the actual problem. Active roof leaks can point us to a definite direction in a minimal amount of time. Something very important to remember is water will only fall one direction, that is down. This is a fact that we may know, but not realize when looking at the over all picture. Since water always travels down hill, it will always follow any lower slope. Any slope in any direction is an opportunity to expand our E over E ratio.

Non-active roof leaks are the worst. Since most people do not deal with roof leaks on a day-to-day basis, they can come up with some unusual leak stories. Some people give no real useful information, or zany explanations at times. It may have simply been a light drip that only dripped eleven times, but for the witness it was pouring in a lot of water, but the same leak maybe considered, not a big deal to others. Depends on whom you talk to.

The point of course is to investigate, investigate and finally investigate again. You may have to look at the same problem twice or three times before you realize something like angled decking is pulling or pushing water to or from a certain location.

Sunken in decking is probably one of the most over looked items on the roof. Many companies put very heavy equipment, materials and units on the decking without the proper support. This causes the decking to bend in, or sink downward. This damage is hard to recognize and permanent. This will be where the path of travel usually stops, or cause a break in the path of travel. This of course results in a roof leak if opportunity presents itself. It's hard to see with the naked eye or even notice until you utilize a hand level or ball barring over the suspected area on top of the roof surface.

Water can travel while avoiding several exit points or opportunities to drain out and down, as it travels along the flutes of decking. The path of travel may pass by an entire edge, but due to sagging decking, the water never leaks out of the edge of the roof.

If you see other rusted, stained areas make notes, always look for what happened at the areas you have not worked on yet with similar problems. These could expose simple commonalities that may direct you into a specific cause and effect scenario.

If I come to your job site, I will probably ask you this question. What is a roof leak? Answer, a roof leak is a roof related problem that has been proven to be a standard roof leak that contains at least one negative indicator. That indicator is negative for Other sources, and positive for at least one or more other indicators. One thing to keep in mind is, to get complete access to the roof related problem, and to all areas between.

Troughing will tell us if a building suffered from roof related problems in the past or present. Perhaps the condition of the roof is great, but there have been problems relating to the units? Maybe there were problems with the drains? Many roofs or buildings have their own unique quarks or commonalities. Some buildings have only window leaks, thats a commonality. Some buildings have never experienced a roof leak. They just replace the roof every ten years as required by budgeting.

Creating a flow chart or taking notes of these commonalities can be valuable. We may have to run a repair for a fellow worker at a place where they may be very familiar. We would have to start from step one to figure out what he or she may just be able to look at and say, "Oh, that happens when water backs up in the sewers. These notes could save someone a lot of misery and time.

Notebook will do just fine. If you are a good record keeper, you probably have your time, date and materials used, all that information on your work order, plus a complete record in a notebook with each customers name separating each account in alphabetical order. We generally call it a Captains Log.

Roof leaks that have developed do much more long term damage and can quietly escalate into a dangerous scenario. In addition, developed roof leaks rarely ever have an E over E ratio of 1:1.

Any time you run into a roof leak scenario, always assume that it did not start yesterday. A developed leak can also be active once every ten years. It may be non-active for years, while all the other components are still in full operation, except an active exit point. Good ventilation may be evaporating the water before the next rain event prevents it from over flowing, but it still has an Entry point, a Reservoir, and Insulation elements, and a Path of travel and it is not related to Other sources.

The more positive indicators you have, the more likely you have a legitimate roof leak. If you have a positive result from Other sources, then you do not have a legitimate roof leak. You can have both, be vigil.

Concrete deck, and layers of roof can prolong or expand the path of travel and may require a lot of water just to prime or saturate the path of travel, that eventually leaks out many feet away from the entry point, because of this there may only be a few drops of water seen at the exit point, while gallons of water are trapped within the roof system and may never make it to the exit point.

We will always start with removing the possibilities of other sources. Take reliable measurements of the exit point(s). Create a search field. Utilize perpendicular and parallel strategies in relation to the decking and insulation. Conduct a trough search. Secure an Entry or entry points, and finally make the necessary repairs, thereby starving all reservoirs and paths of travel off permanently. In turn extinguishing the roof related problem. Wow, sounds like a lot of stuff. That's what this book is about. To give you any kind of help in searching is my only goal.

Some of us are ordered to get on the roof without having the opportunity to see any possible activity inside. Maybe the building is locked, or no one can find the key. You will however, learn to utilize these strategies and may no longer need access to the area under an average size roof to make great repairs. Impossible? Hardly.

Residuals from chapter 3

There are six indicators that confirm or deny a legitimate roof leak or relation or an item related to Other sources.

Indicator 1 Elimination of Other Sources. If negative, legitimate roof leak.

Indicator 2 Identified exit point(s), if positive most likely roof related.

Indicator 3 Identify a Paths of Travels, if positive most likely roof related.

Indicator 4 Identify any reservoirs, if positive most likely roof related.

Indicator 5 Identify any and all Entry points, if positive most likely roof related.

Indicators are either positive or negative.

For each indicator there are variables.

Variables are measurements/unknowns that you will have on site.

Negative indicators can prove that a roof related problem is <u>not</u> legitimate.

There are two types of roof leaks, sudden or established.

Active means that the leak is currently dripping.

Non-active or in-active means the leak was active, but isn't at this time.

All roofs have commonalities.

Chapter 4

Elimination of Other Sources

Eliminating "Other Sources," is the first and most critical step in determining whether you are dealing with a legitimate roof leak or something that relates to other sources such as non-roof related items. Like all indicators, it will be positive or negative.

A positive indication that we have a non-roof related problem that directly ties to other sources in the picture above. When the wind blew the heavy rain the right direction, they had a terrible leak. This indication was positive for Other sources, which means for this particular problem everything else cancels out 99%. This would be a 100% determination for a typical roof repair person, don't be tricked. Water can drain from the pipe and roof. As you can see the pipe has been damaged, maybe the roof has been too. Never take rare possibilities for granted. Its might be some what rare, but does happen.

Categorically speaking there are "Other Source," related items that can be traced back to; HVAC units, pipes, drain pipes, penetrations, brick walls, antenna hook ups, dog boxes, coping metal, edge metals, supports, etc. These items are not roof related, but can be very convincing when imitating a roof leak. Matter of fact, some of these non-roof related items may become active during a rain event only because they are associated with high humidity or high dew points, or maybe high winds. Even a sudden pressure change during a thunderstorm will pull water into a building in an unusual manner.

Even though there maybe a typical rain event, what makes it unusual, if there may be high winds associated with the weather event which may activate unusual non-roof related problems of all types and may seem not unusual. These unusual items may list from wind/rain blowing in through windows, doors or door jams. Concrete, bricks and siding can sometimes drain/weep water through a structure in an unusual way that looks exactly like a legitimate roof leak from the right view. On closer examination of exactly what is going on, one can make a education decision as to what is exactly going on.

What is roof related and what is not? Another very important question. A new roof and all the fixings is all a building needs in theory. When the expression is utilizes such as all the fixings, we mean, penetrations, drains installed properly and the edging attached/coping basically a complete roof. However, the roof is complete already on the roll. All material that is on a roll that is attached over insulation is the roof, all attachments to, around and through is not roof related, period! This is huge and very powerful information.

This can make the difference between eight hour job for two men that won't stop a roof leak, compared to an informed repair specialist who realized that the proper repair can be made with a small amount of metal primer and a good industrial caulk in a couple hours including travel time, clean up and meeting with happy customers and a predictable and easier process.

A chimney may be a great suspect for an unsolved non-roof related problem. A broken windowsill or maybe a small hairline crack somewhere within a concrete wall around the parameter of the roof. They too are categorized, as other sources. The result may be the same but the cause is very different.

Besides sprinkler/fire or plumbing, there can also be condensation that travels through concrete or sweating drainpipes not properly insulated. Clogged gutter edges, water heads, down spouts backing up with water, almost everything we generally take for granite can create a non-roof related problem.

Here are a few examples of real life roof leaks that were not roof related. Even though there are only a few examples, they cover the basics of O.S.

A good example of eliminating other source caused leaks, in the picture above. High winds pulled back the 14 gauge metal cap that was secured with sheet metal screws. Notice the rust? This item never leaked inside, but you can see that this cap has been collecting moisture and rusting for many years. We wondered how many people have stood on this dead and weakened penetration, and did not fall through this three-story building to their deaths.

This is one of those things you do not know about until you see it for yourself. This is why you should never be afraid to take these items apart. Warning: Do not take apart items that cannot be put back together. We found three other caps taking in water, but not actively leaking to the floor.

The customer seen the pictures and was very impressed. You must understand, this is four roof leak calls that have been eliminated in one trip. Got some sweet repair work out of that for a day too. As much as possible, show the customer the problems you prevent in the future and the big time savings you can generate.

In the picture above, we have poorly sealed power supply lines at the bottom of this HVAC unit. As many of you may know under this HVAC unit are large cut outs through the decking where water can easily drip out of. This was an instant red flag because this was over a brand new roof. They also had 6 other units sealed up the same way. The others weren't leaking enough through the system to be visibly active down stairs at the time of our emergency call. This problem is directly tied to, other sources.

Drilling holes to run power supply lines through the bottom of any unit is always bad. When you see it, report it to someone. This practice causes a lot problems and can cost a lot money. If power lines are not running through the wall of the unit to the outside wall of the penetration or a dog box, it will eventually leak.

Small or mini water heaters around office kitchen areas are a good example of other sources. Often these mini water heaters will be put into a wooden cabinet at floor level causing an active leak over the tenant down below or even two stories below. Sometimes of course, these mini water heaters can be hidden above the ceiling tiles or drop ceiling space over head just under the decking.

You would be surprised how many people may occupy a building, and never know about some of the things just over their heads. These problems of course are easy to eliminate if you properly search them out to their source. Always have stepladders and do not forget to take pictures, every step of the way.

In some rare cases, other source type leaks can be identified easily because the leak is active when there is an absence of a rain event. When you know you have not had any rain in a while and you know there is not a cut, hole or problem with the membrane/roof, you can feel confident that you have a problem with plumbing, condensation or a faulty HVAC unit. Maybe a clogged J-trap.

Do not be surprised if you have to prove it. You may have to prove it with a Water Test with Time Differentials, covered in Chapter 16. Again, always have a digital camera and take shots of the problem/staining or active trails of water as it is occurring. Remember, anyone can put down a patch; the main job is to trouble shoot a problem to its source and being able to prove it with photos and a positive end result with no more activity.

Frost from a malfunctioning HVAC unit in the picture above. Notice the displaced gravel? Several repair people attempted to find the problem with no luck. We figured quickly there was no problem with the roof. Anytime you have high humidity, and a poor performing HVAC unit, you will get non-roof related problems that can mimic a roof leak. Most typical causes are excessive freezing and not enough evaporation, then sudden melting, creating intermittent heavy leaking and over flowing the drain pan especially if the J-trap might be a little clogged, which as the water drips out it will drip out cold or very cool inside the building at the exit point. This actually had a Zero path of travel with water that was cold enough to drink.

These types of leaks become more active when the humidity and dew points are high. Usually when this happens, it often rains. Just coincidental that both the unit freezes up and it rains about the same time. This will cause many to think it is a roof leak, always make sure you inspect all penetrations and units in close proximity of the reported issue.

Make sure you pay attention to a particular unit if you are suspicious of one malfunctioning. An indicator that you maybe dealing with a malfunction HVAC unit is the motor runs non-stop, or never runs. If summer time, expect the units to run off and on/cycle all day. Eventually HVAC units stop running when the inside temperature has been met. You may be able to notice that other units may have switched on and off automatically, yet one in particular keeps running without a break or running loudly or making unusual sounds. Or appears to be resetting constantly.

Always have a camera ready before you open up what you may thing is a malfunctioning HVAC unit. When the permafrost-ice melts, your evidence is lost and it goes fast. Opening an access panel and identifying a large iceberg or frozen coils within the system can cause the temperature inside to equalize with the outside temperature and the permafrost melts at an accelerated rate. Better get pictures quickly, before your evidence vanishes before your eyes.

Above we have a better look at frozen coils and hardware within the HVAC unit. We were the fifth company to check this problem out, but the first to solve it. After opening the unit, the permafrost evaporated in about 2 minutes. The ice took much longer as it was four to six inches thick. HVAC people we spoke to told us to leave it along and let nature take its course.

We did not make any repairs, we just simply took pictures and replaced the door. HVAC guy said it had a blown compressor or something. We don't know, were repair guys by trade right? Some customers will expect you to fix some of these items. Don't do it.

Your trade is roofing, not HVAC work, or plumbing and so on, unless trained for that particular field don't do it. Earlier in this book there were mentioning about how many other trades that a roof repair specialist actually have to be trained or some understanding in.

There are minor and major repairs for just about everything. Sometimes we can add a Sheet metal/tech screw to a missing area on a HVAC unit. We can also add new weather stripping to prevent water from being pulled in with a little bit of caulk. This sometimes happens when a larger motor is installed in a unit and a roof related problem becomes active because the strong vacuum is pulling water during the rain event into the unit. Sometimes, and only sometimes weather stripping added along the door panels can cure this. Cheaper than another motor install. Always refrain from caulking or altering HVAC units as much as possible. Leave that to the HVAC people.

Below we had a terrible leak on this built-up roof. This roof leaked when the water got high enough to get into some wall flashing. We found the drain clogged up from gravel and asphalt. A roof is designed to take on a certain amount of water, when there is too much, you have leaks. Even though it was a roof and it was a drain that was clogged up with asphalt and gravel, they were still forced to call a plumber.

Lets talk briefly about Fire sprinkler heads. In all my years as a roof repair guy I have never seen one fail. Any and every time I have had a roof leak it has always been a plumbing problem leading up to the sprinkler head. It just so happens the sprinkler head is at the bottom end of the pipe at the drop ceiling level, while the main line or water supply line is up above. When there is a pipe leak, it is usually small, and constant. If there were a problem with the sprinkler head, it would explode with water.

This free image was collected from the web. This sprinkler is the typical fire sprinkler head you will see in most businesses. Remember when you see dirty staining, or water ceiling pads/tiles there could very well be an issue with the plumbing. Complete investigation into the matter is necessary.

Removal of ceiling pads are always necessary when investigating any roof leak. Some people, assume and lose. Set up the step ladders, lay out the plastic and remove the pads and investigate the matter completely. Confirm there is not water leaking from any other source, take lots of pictures from many different angles. For you so called photographers out there, think again. For the customer, seeing your photos, they expect a story or a story line of what you found, what you fixed and what it looks like now. One picture of each step of the phase can be a disaster, as one or two of those photos may not turn out well. Maybe blurry, or maybe your finger over the lens. When your in a hurry, you never know. Take many photos, close, further away, left/right, etc. This is how we prove our case.

Of course if it is not raining outside during your leak call, and there is no other water dripping from the ceiling area, you need not set up your tall ladder or get roof access. This is due to those circumstances, and these circumstances only. For instance, if it were raining, and there were water leaking near by the fire sprinkler system, you must set up your tall ladder or access the roof. But! But, if you took only ten minutes to get there, and it took you only about ten minutes to find that this is only a plumbing issue, access the roof and look it over and check in with the customer. Do not look for work to be done, look for serious issues only! Check in and out with the customer, if you found nothing substantial, let them know you solved the roof related problem which was non-roof related and did check over the roof and found no serious or new issues. Show them your photos, fill out paper work.

Penetrations are often the cause of leaks that are related to items that are not roof related. Most penetrations are often made to specifications that prevent them from taking in water. There can be circumstances that cause penetrations to leak. A good example is the short penetration in the photo above. Notice it is only three inches of height above roof surface. When heavy monsoon rains appear, this penetration leaks terribly. Even the rain skirt on the stack next to the penetration, notice the old deteriorated caulk.

The only solution for this issue is to add height to the top of the penetration with more wood and re-wrap the upper part of the penetration and replace the vent/fan.

When you know that you have eliminated the possibility that the roof related problem is not caused by other sources, then and only then, can you move on to the other indicators.

Residuals from chapter 4

Your first and most critical factor/indicator associated with a roof/non-roof related problem is the elimination of Other sources.

Other sources, is where a non-roof related leak is caused by other means than the roof membrane or adjoining cured and uncured flashings.

Non-roof related items may include:

Condensation issues.

Pipes, plumbing.

Sprinkler systems.

Overhead mini water heaters.

Windows/doors or entrance ways.

Cracks in concrete along walls, chimneys or even failed mortar.

Large chillers, pumping apparatuses, etc.

Metal flashings.

Penetrations.

Water heads, drains.

Heating or cooling systems that are either malfunctioning or not properly installed are main causes of false positives when searching for a roof leak.

Ask about other non-roof related problems in the past that may have caused a similar problem.

Always use ladders or lifts when investigating for O.S.

Do not assume what a problem could be until its been fully investigated, and vise-a-versa.

If problem is HVAC related and you can prove it with Water Testing with time differentials (Chapter 16), recommend that the customer call their HVAC Service Company for service or correct the non-roof related issue.

Sometimes if a plumbing issue is the problem the water will feel very warm or very cool. Digital thermometer while collecting the water in a vessel/container is a must. This can also be a strong indication of steam pipe related issue.

If the problem is mortar around chimneys, cracks along concrete walls related issue and you can prove it with Water Testing with time differentials (Chapter 16), recommend that the customer call a concrete contractor.

If the problem is from windowsills or windows in general, recommend that the customer contact a window contractor.

Do not do work that is clearly intended for other trades. Do not attempt repairs at plumbing, electrical and windows or concrete. Leave these to the professionals. Besides this generates work for the other people. Sometimes they also generate work for us. Staying separate binds us together in the end.

Chapter 5

Exit Points

Dripping water, or water dripping out of the ceiling area of a building is generally called a roof leak and can be an illusion of sorts if not properly understood or investigated. Repair personnel know them as Exit Points.

One of the very and easily identifiable indicator or factors is the exit point, once located it will be the anchor of your investigation. Water will be exiting from decking or the basic structure above your head down onto a ceiling tile when called out on most roof leak calls. We refrain from calling these unfavorable traces drips/roof leaks initially because we know its only part of the equation and only the end result. Ironic that the last part of a roof leak, is the first thing you identify. This is mainly why roof repairs are so difficult, we have to work the total equation backwards. It is like working in a mirror, behind the scenes with hidden solutions.

Before we move onto what a exit point is lets quickly go over what an exit point is not. In the photo at the beginning of this chapter shows ceiling tile staining from a previous roof leak. Many repairmen/women make the age old mistake of not removing the ceiling tiles and not looking at what is on the other side of that pad. Oh sure, it will give you a point of reference over all if you just simply measure out from the stain, but what if it isn't a roof leak at all? That is a huge what if. Please take the time to remove the ceiling tiles or pads and inspect what is exactly going on inside the system by removing the possibility of other sources. Don't assume that the ceiling tile is the exit point, it is not.

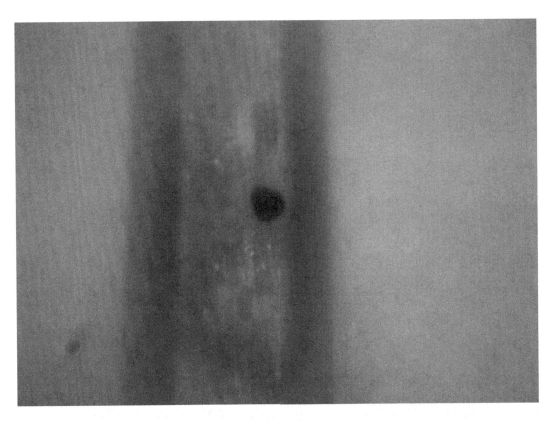

Above is the top view of an actual exit point. A typical blow hole burned through metal decking. The welder/metal worker hit the beam on the second or lower weld but hit only air on the upper weld leaving an opening that will allow water to drain out during a rain event if the opportunity presents itself in the future, resulting in an active exit point/roof leak. Notice the small fastener hole at the left top part of the upper rib. This cuts down on the amount of exit points that can exist in the flute or channel/bottom half of the deck.

That's just the beginning, end laps and penetrations which of course make more exit points must be take into consideration as well. In essence, an exit point is any location where water can drain or drip out of at the structured deck section of the roof combination that pertains to tracking the motion of water from the exit point back to the entry point.

End laps of decking, penetrations, drop ceiling hangers are the most common scenarios for many exit points where you will see water draining or dripping directly out of most of the time however, the laps of metal decking are often hidden from sight because they always sit on a beam or support of some type. Besides you cannot have metal decking not supported by anything or over lapping and just sticking out beyond the support beam, which some of us have seen it happen maybe by a couple of inches, regardless of the rarities exit points associated with metal decking can happen along any edge of the material, any opening cut in to it

Exception to the rule:

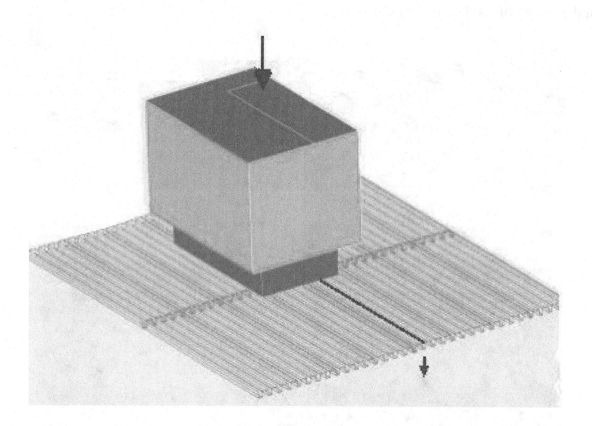

When its not roof related; Occasionally you may have an HVAC unit allowing water in to an exit point location/area that mimics a roof leak by leaking onto the metal decking while channeling and traveling to a typical or any other possible exit point. In the illustration above it is simply draining off of the lap of the deck. This is a rare scenario, but does happen. In my home made diagram of a HVAC unit on top of metal decking, its easy to see without the insulation how water can fall straight down within the parameter of the unit down onto the deck. The cut out in the deck directly under the unit is usually big enough for duct work only, so there is often more than enough decking left in place under the unit that will allow water to travel. Confirmation and separation of the two are discussed in Chapter 16.

Roofs and exit points cannot exist unless you have decking of some type. Regardless of the type of decking you have on hand, there will always be a way for the water to travel through or around it. Either the water will run out of decking and drain off the edge or it will drip out of a hole or rusted/damaged area of the deck. There are very specific rules that control how water acts once inside the roof at this last step just before physical and visual activation.

Decking comes in all types of sizes and shapes and manufactured from several types of materials. Basically different lengths, heights and widths to meet any need. Decking comes in different thickness from light weight to heavy duty. Below is the typical metal decking you will see often.

The photo above from Japan, shows that even in different countries they often run decking parallel to the longest wall. This is important information for you. By nature you can imagine that if you have long walls, the decking will run with the walls direction. Don't be surprised if people do the opposite. Sometimes that happens, but for the most part you can depend on the direction of your decking to run the same direction of your longest wall. Can you see the exit points in the photo above? Yes, those yellowish/greenish marks are weld marks. Each one is a potential exit point. Don't forget that each and every edge and every lap also is an exit point.

Below a cartoon drawing of metal decking. How many exit points are there? This is decking without mechanical fasteners.

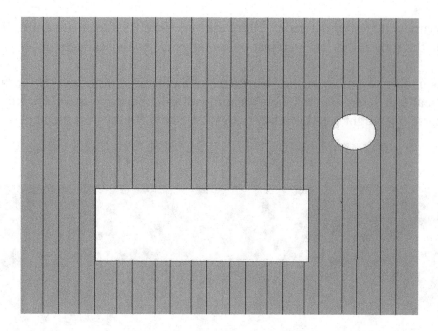

To keep it simple, every lap of the decking, every weld hole/blow hole, every edge and every fastener/screw hole or penetration openings are exit points.

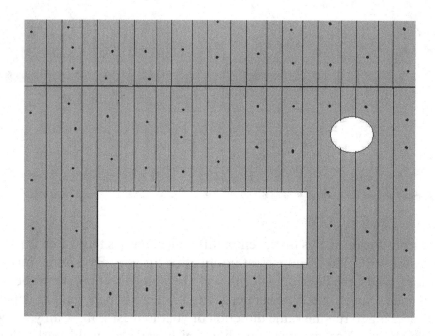

In the drawing above, we have a more realistic look. This is the same decking with holes to represent mechanical fasteners. Notice that they will be on the upper, or rib part of the decking. Sometimes, you can have applicators, accidentally put a fastener through the flute or deep part of the channel if the fasteners are long enough which sometimes they will pull back out and move over after they realize they hit in the general wrong location. Not often, but sometimes.

If you look at metal decking from head on, it looks like the drawing below, basically.

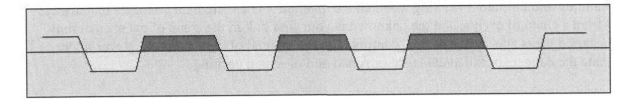

The upper parts of the decking divided by a line colored in orange are the ribs. The ribs are the part of the decking that the insulation will lay on and be mechanically attached to as well.

The bottom halves of the decking marked in beige are known as the flutes/channels. This part of the decking will lay on beams/joists and will carry the water long distances depending on slope and direction of the laps in relation to that particular slope and angle of the flow of water within the system.

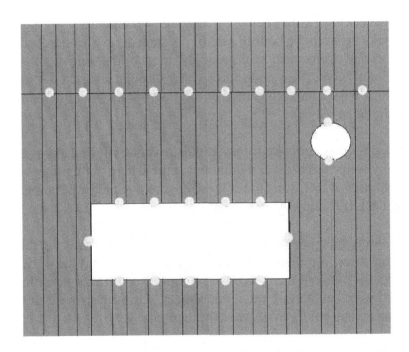

Marked with yellow we have twenty-four possible exit points, not counting the outer edges. It seems like a lot and it is a lot. This example shows you where water would or could leak from on a simple layer of metal decking. Any cut out, flute or lap is always a possible exit point.

Always look for weak decking and walk cautiously on buildings you have not been to before. You never know how old the decking is or if there was some unknown damage that you or a member of your crew may find or step through by accident. Several times over the years we have uncovered openings where insulation was put over a 2 foot by 2 foot opening and nothing else.

Some openings larger, many smaller we discovered the hard way. At least enough to almost break an ankle or tear a ligament, or possibly rip through the membrane and slide through into the building and fall into a working wood chuck machine. There are many dangers that always lead from a chain of events, and the unknown is your first link in the chain of events that may have started years ago, and your now coming onto the tail end of it, be careful! Never under estimate the dangers of failed/damaged or rotted and/or rusted decking.

Let's look at concrete decking. Most concrete decks are prefabricated now a days. Usually when one looks up from the bottom side of decking or up at concrete decking they may see large control joints and even cracks. Surprisingly, most of the time these are only cosmetic in nature. It takes a lot of work, pressure to force water through concrete. Much more so then metal or wood decking. Like a parking garage or old in ground swimming pool, a concrete deck pretty much works the same way.

Water being one of the most destructive forces in the universe will find a way to work through concrete if there is any weakness at all and drain out some where. Often that course will be long and very enduring. Matter of fact, sometimes these concrete related exit points will create stalactites under the deck if leaking long enough.

As the water travels through the system or concrete, it breaks down the minerals and disperses these mineral as a stalactites. You will not see them under any other type of deck, and you will not see them often but they are out there. Rest assured they could take years to develop. The ones I have witnessed were soft almost like a thick slush, semi-transparent. It was an off white, almost a dirty looking crystal color. Wish we kept them.

Of all the decking in the world, concrete will always conceal the actual true location but can give you a general location of an entry point in relation to the exit point. We will get to that later.

Where does the water drain through?

Notice the yellow lines, which is where water can seep through. Along with edges and cracks, penetrations will also allow water to drain through the deck like in the photo below.

Above is the bottom side of a solid concrete deck. There were no stress joints installed and only one penetration on the entire roof and you are looking at it. The roof was completely saturated and ruined but it only leaked in a very small amount of water though the deck itself.

There is also another commonly used type decking. This decking looks like spaghetti and some type of resin. This decking usually comes in two foot by four-foot slabs and lies directly on metal tracking. Water drains almost straight through this decking. Usually a 1:1 over all ratio with this decking.

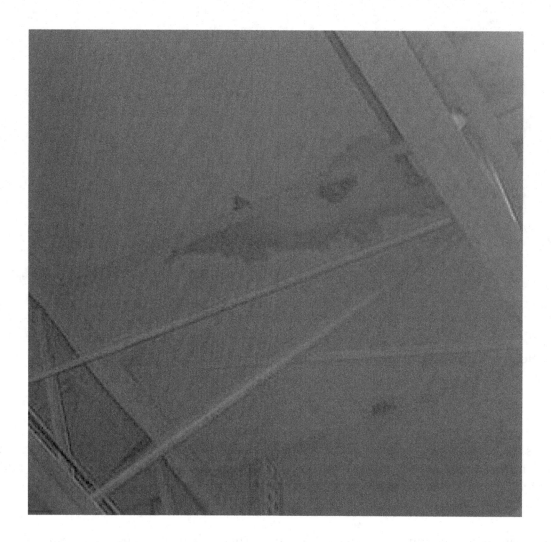

This decking is called Gypsum. Instead of water going around the material itself, it goes directly through. Because there is no traveling for the water possible once the water falls down from the insulation level to the deck, there will be no path of travel associated with this type of decking unless there is a vapor barrier securely over the gypsum decking. Typically, the water staining or exit point you see below will usually be directly under your entry point.

Gypsum does not absorb water but wood will absorb some moisture. Wood deck is usually put down with a standard treated and tongue and groove design. This usually makes it pretty much water resistant. As the years go by, it will cure or flash off and will begin absorbing water.

Most wooden decks are tongue and groove and will not allow water to drain through easily if put together properly. Typically, water can drain out of each tongue and groove lap of the wood and any loose knots or cracks in the wood, especially after the wood has had few years or so of aging.

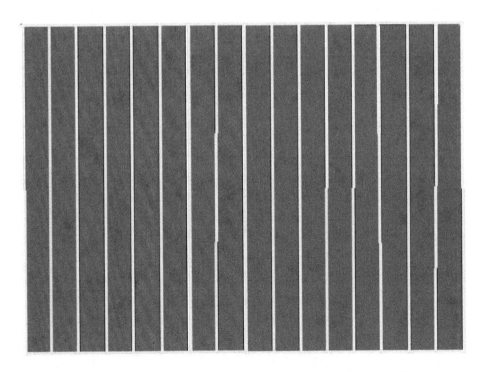

Above a hand drawn diagram of the many possible exit points that are associated with a wooden deck. Because wooden decks are so well put together by design and by the craftsmen that put them down, actual exit points are few. Regardless, theses are the real world possibilities.

Residuals from chapter 5

An exit point is water that drains or drips directly out of decking.

An exit point is the second factor/indicator that you could have a legitimate roof leak.

Exit points give us exact measurements that are directly tied to the path of travel which sometimes can be an arrow pointing us back to the entry point.

Exit points can be found at end laps of decking.

Exit points can be found at cutouts for penetrations.

Exit points can be created by mechanical fasteners or by nails.

Exit points can also be the holes drop ceiling installers make, at the bottom halves of the decking while installing hangers.

Exit points can produce stalactites under concrete decking.

Gypsum decking allows water to flow directly through.

Many exit points in one area or a relatively small area is referred to as Spider webbing.

Chapter 6

Paths of Travel

There are three direct paths of travel associated with a roof and non-roof related leaks. Two related to roof leaks, one related to non-roof related activity. Paths of travel are very fundamental and only do what gravity, water and slope require.

The first is what is known as the Hard path of travel. The hard path is always associated with decking. Metal, wood and concrete or gold it does not matter, if the decking is made out of egg shells, that hard path of travel is tied to a hard shell deck. There is never an exception to these rules.

The second path of travel is the Soft path of travel. Named soft path simply because of the fact it is tied directly to insulation and vapor barriers only. This path of travel will cross over/through insulation or will either absorb or deflect water at a much lower rate or distance that is not related to decking in any way. In other words, the distance associated with the soft path of travel will rarely ever be over 30 feet in length, while the distance associated with the hard path of travel can be hundreds of feet in length.

Finally the third path of travel known as the Zero path of travel. Identified as zero because this is an all out drain or drip from inside of a non-roof related item that hits bottom without making any contact with insulation/decking while passing through the roof structure.

For instance, the path of travel will lead in from a unit/penetration and by-pass insulation, decking and drip/drain straight through to the floor/ground. Zero path of travel is always associated with Other Sources.

Either way, those paths of travel that channel water are originating from an entry point that is coming from somewhere and going somewhere, supplying water like a small river to an exit point.

Often un-locatable roof leaks will have a very long path of travel. Rather than taking into consideration that the possibility of a long distance path is even possible.

There is also the possibility that there could be layers of what appears to be like a fire rated dry wall application that have been put down here and there over the years on top of certain heavy duty decking. This is to be treated the same as insulation or with the same rules as a water resistant insulation, it is not however water resistant. Usually this material absorbs water but at a very slow rate as it may take many years to soak a one foot by one foot square area. Before water actually soaks through or goes around these types of barriers, water will travel beyond or over them depending on the slope. Thereby, extending our path of travel even more so.

Water sometimes will fuse metal together with oxidation, which will not allow water through where it once flow easily before. Every rain event, adds more water and more rust in some cases. A path of travel 10' to15' feet, or 3.5 meters is normal for the average roof leak. Oxidized laps, debris laying in the bottom of the flutes/channels of the decking with uneven sloping and its not hard to see how far and endlessly water can travel. Remember, all of this is hidden away from sight in most cases because laps of decking are almost always hidden on top of beams/joists and the bottom side of decking is often painted.

The weight of the water will cause sloping or a change in the slope, in most cases. R factor breaks down and the lay of the roof or change the flow of water off the roof. These unusual circumstances add to the roof related problem process beyond typical or normal standards and are usually active on an average of 4 to 8 years before being discovered and relief is given with the proper repair.

Exactly the channel of decking where the water is dripping or draining out, is exactly your path of travel. Just like a treasure map this is part of your direction back to the entry point.

Most assume that the entry point will be immediately over or exactly directly over the exit point. Fact is, in many cases the entry point and exit points for most roof leaks will be within a reasonable distance from each other due to chance/luck and the specific building materials combined with what of type of rain event that proceeds the initial roof related problem. Very rarely will the exit point and entry point align perfectly together. Let's take a look at home hand drawn metal decking.

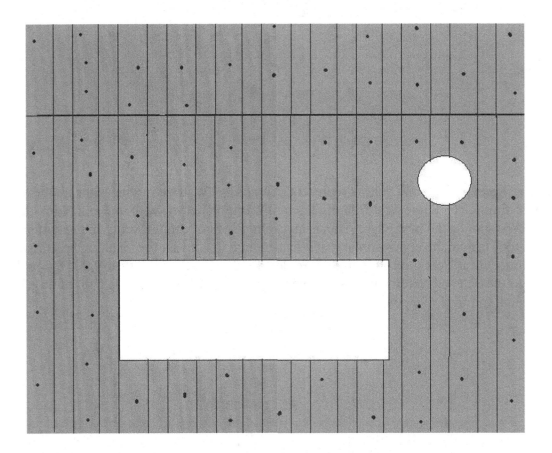

Notice all the fastener holes are all on the top (rib) part of the decking. Most installers intentionally try to hit the rib part of the deck.

This prevents the possibility of accidentally sending a mechanical faster through electrical or plumbing structures below with catastrophic results. Another reason is we need shorter fasteners to hit the tops of the ribs. Shorter fasteners make life easier for roofers/applicators.

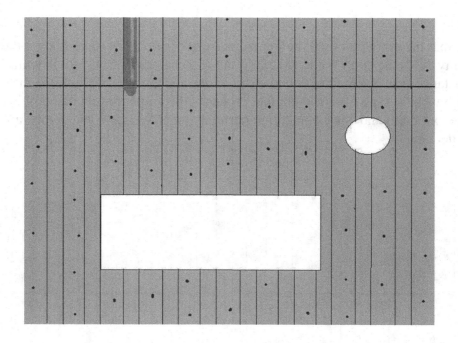

The blue represents water and yellow represent exit points. Water lying in a flute above. Most likely tight fitting lap. Same tight fighting lap in illustration below, with one exit point identified by the yellow spot on the next page. This is an example of not enough water in the system to activate a roof leak in the upper drawing and just enough to active a roof leak in the drawing below. Notice its at a cut out. How many people would believe automatically that the problem is related to the unit and never solve the problem? This would not be a Zero path of travel. This is a Hard path of travel.

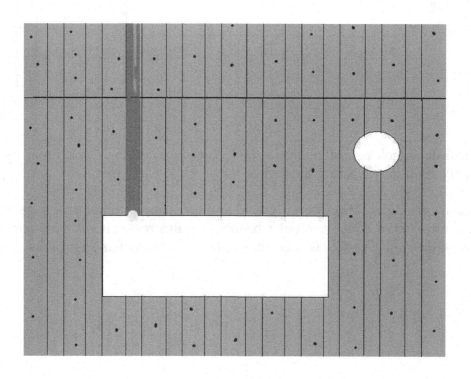

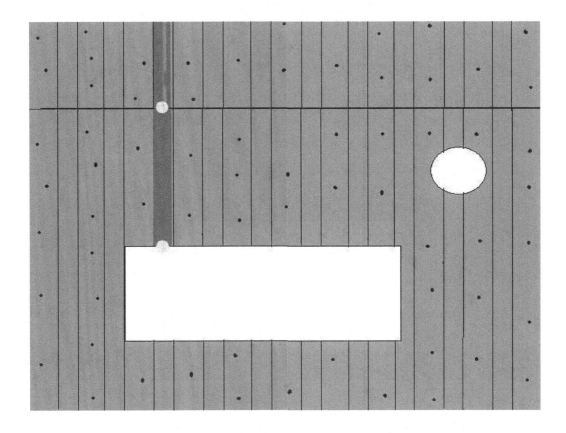

In the illustration above, we have one path of travel and two exit points that are identified by the yellow. This scenario tells us three things. First, it identifies the hard path of travel. Secondly, it tells us the laps of the decking are loosely laid. Water that is dripping at the cut out with water dripping out of the lap near by absolutely nails the path of travel. Anytime you have two or more drips in the same line along decking, that is a confirmed path of travel and that is an solid compass point. That is real direction.

It's also not hard to understand that if it began leaking under this cut out, most of us would assume there was a problem with the unit. We in fact, could be on the opposite end of the leak; this is why we need to identify the path of travel. This path not only tells us where the water exits out, it gives us direction to where its coming from.

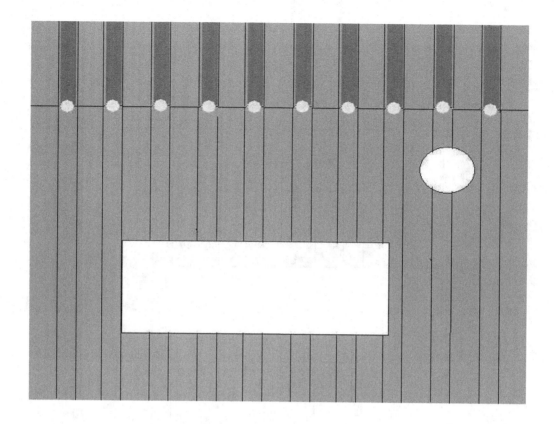

The difference a tight or loosing fitting lap can make. Loose fitting lap in Illustration above.
Tight fitting laps below makes a huge difference in the length of the path of travel. Notice how
the water passed over the tight fitting laps and went on to the other exit points around the cut
outs in the drawing below.

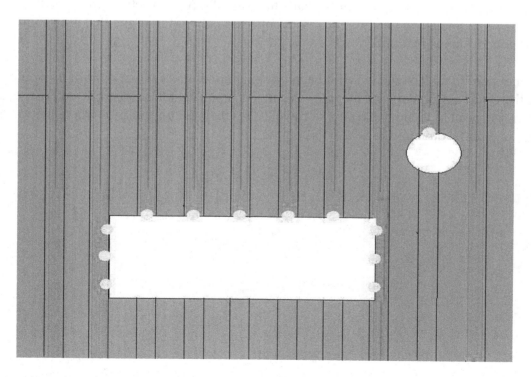

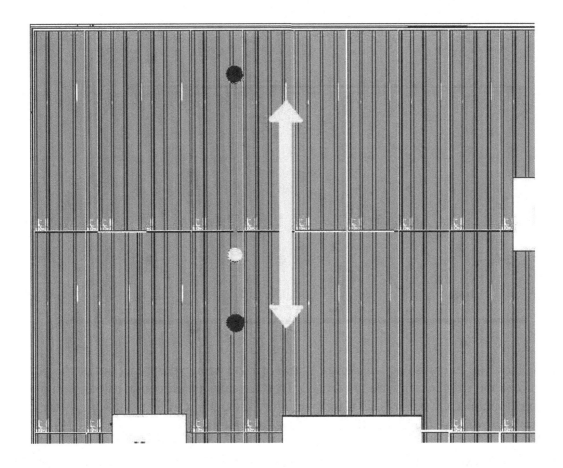

In illustration above, we see two exit points marked in black and an entry point marked in yellow on the blue line. As you can see by the two-ended yellow arrow that the water has entered in and has expanded, in both directions until exit points have been found. In this illustration, black markers are over vacant fastener holes.

The height of the water inside the flute of the decking can reach a height of a couple of inches before finding an exit point on a typical decked roof because of the bottom channels and sagging.

Let us look at sloped metal decking. Remember, the slope tells us where to take our search in addition, by where it's coming from.

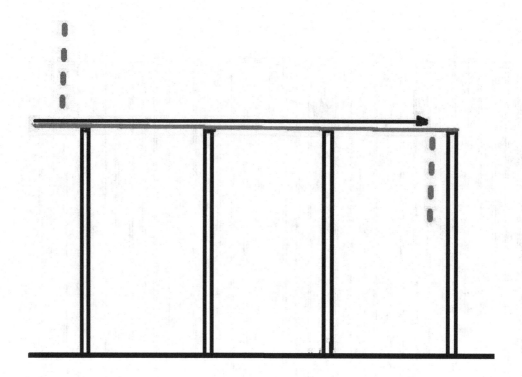

Illustration above is general sloped decking. Water or H2O depicted in blue, notice the black line on top over the red decking with the arrow. This indicates the direction of our path of travel. In some construction, each beam is set lower per every set amount of feet. As long as the metal deck laps point down hill, the leak will always travel beyond the lap.

If there are no any exit points, or holes in the decking in that particular flute, water may travel until it runs out of decking or the end/wall. It may travel from the very front of the building, to the very rear of the building or side-to-side. Again this commonly seen scenario, cross lateral circulation.

This is where our mini hand level and ball bearing come into play. Some roofs look perfectly flat, but are not. This may have to do with the way the insulation appears to lay. This can be confirmed by selecting areas on the roof to test for the fall or slope of the roof.

A ball barring will show the over all slope and the mini hand level is for the bottom side of the decking. Use that hand level to show the slope of the decking. The main reason for the path of travel is that is connects definite points of a roof leak into one body.

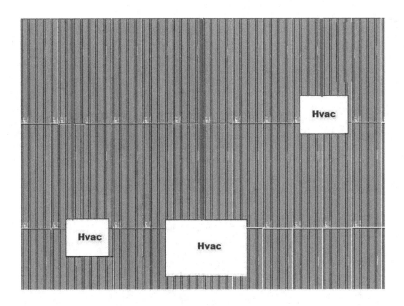

This illustration shows three paths of travel that is traveling from the front of the building down to the units. Again, this is easily misunderstood that there is a problem at the unit and not the roof. Why? Because we only see the water dripping out of the bottom side of the decking under the penetrations. Always take this possibility into consideration.

What you cannot see can kill your success rate; however, understanding how this variable relates to the roof can make all the difference. Rather than only making repairs at the units, you will track straight back or uphill.

Another reality is decking that runs one direction and adjoining decking that runs the opposite direction. This is Bi-directional decking.

This often happens in a valley area, but can happen anywhere on the roof. If you move around a large facility, you may find several different locations with decking running different directions.

This will cause a great sense of confusion about exactly where the water is running from. That is why it so important to identify what direction the decking your working on is, because this direction can suddenly change for various unknown reasons. If you pay attention to this information, it will lead you to something good.

What will make it so difficult is that sometimes bi-directional decking will lay at its lowest point over an I-beam. This I-beam can also carry water far away to another location, and lead you on a wild goose chase. This is why we should use a ladder or have a lift, so that way we know exactly where the path of travel actually is located by seeing it for ourselves.

Also decking will not over lap in a perpendicular manner. They will lay side-by-side but never over lap like a T-joint. Once in a great while, one directional layer of decking will run right up under a small lip of decking running the opposite direction. Less than 1%.

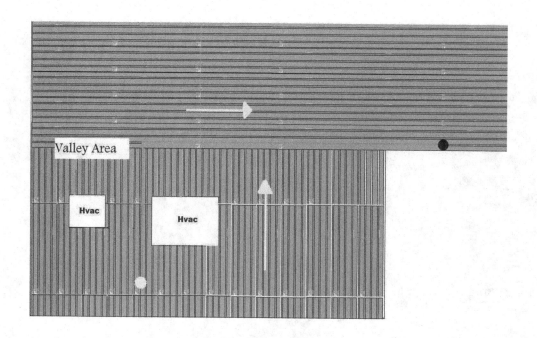

This scenarios is very rare. When decking does slightly t-bone into another slab of decking, water can carry on in a perpendicular direction. Notice how the water travels down from the yellow mark to the valley area. Then it falls into another flute from other decking, and with the slope of the roof, water travels perpendicular.

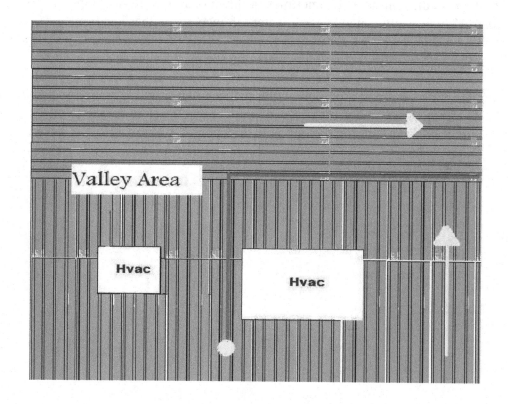

That covers what seems to be the endless list of the path of travel associated with decking. We have covered sloped, flat and loose as well as other possible scenarios when it comes to this basic but most important ingredient of an actual roof leak as it exists. Lets look at the soft path of travel.

The Soft path of travel as mentioned before only deals with insulation, vapor barriers and fire rating materials.

The soft path of travel is influenced by several things. First and foremost is the type of insulation. Some insulation absorbs water some does not. Either way, no matter how much water insulation can absorb, there will always be a flow over. Flow over is simply the process of water once entering into the system through the membrane whether that be by a cut, slice or tear, after water gets in it will lay on the insulation directly under the membrane. This water will flow to a corner or edge of insulation.

Two things will happen. Either water will fall between the cracks of the insulation and continue down to other layers or to the decking, or because the insulation was kicked tightly by the original installers, the path of water will travel beyond the edges of the insulation. This may continue on a sloped roof for quite a distance. Most I have seen has been about 30 feet in length. It was also associated with a very bad roof leak.

You will have thee basic kinds of insulation regardless of the roof. Most popular is fiberglass based products. Insulation comes in two by four foot sheets or 2'x4' and four foot by eight foot or 8'x4'.

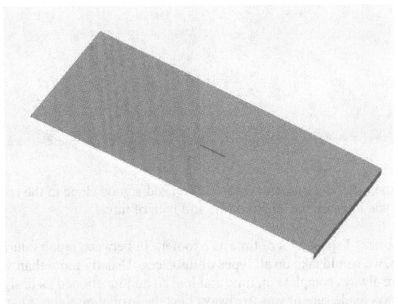

Above my drawing of a 4'x8' sheet of fiberglass based insulation. Some may say that fiberglass will not absorb water. The fiber glass does not absorb the water per say, it can become water logged. Typically if you pour water over the insulation, it will deflect off of the surface and continue to the edge pointing down to the lowest slope. As mentioned before, if the sheets of insulation are kicked tightly together, the edges will not contain its movement to one sheet of material, but instead may move two, three or more sheets across before the water will drain down to the deck level. This soft path of travel can cause an offset. It can direct you in the wrong direction if you are not paying attention. A typical roof leak will have; 1 entry point, one single soft path of travel, one hard path of travel, etc, and the soft path will often be your grey area. To counter act this we conduct Trough Searches. We discuss that more in Advanced Search Techniques.

If you could see inside and under the membrane under the actual cut/hole or slice and look directly at the insulation, this is typically in the drawing below is what you would see typically. Water that traveled to the edge of the insulation and fell down through the cracks down onto the insulation. This is of course the most easiest and most fundamental case scenario.

Depicted in blue, the water does not travel far. If you add a good slope to the recipe and tightly kicked insulation, you increase the length of the soft path of travel.

Roofers will be roofers. I spent a lot of time as a roofer. In between repairs during nice weather with nothing to do, we would take on all types of disasters. Usually more than we could handle. However they were always complete on time and looked and functioned as designed. One thing that my crews always made sure of was to always kick the insulation tight. I caught myself doing it too much. Often we would have sore ankles from kicking insulation constantly as it went down. Lord help us if we had to pull a piece out, it would be almost impossible.

There is nothing wrong with this practice as it does make the R-factor much more efficient and saves a lot of money. It an take the path of travel off course. This is where the exit point an the exit point may run a rye.

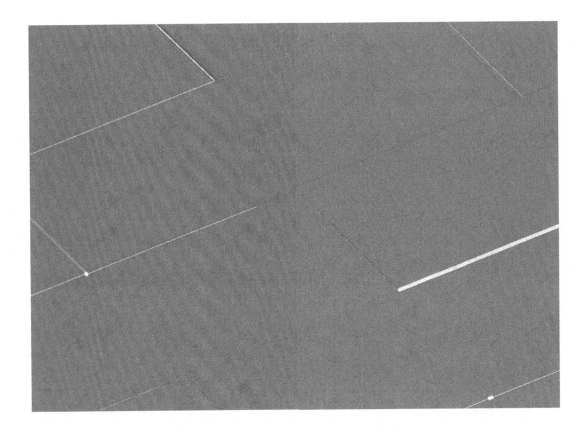

Included above is a drawing of water on top of insulation after entering by means of an entry point directly through the membrane. Notice the water will typically follow the edges of the insulation. Zig-Zag motion is not unusual when you have this circumstance which is more common than one might think.

You will not really know until you walk around on the roof how tight or loose the insulation is, and this is usually learned with experience. After a while you will recognize that certain companies and people do things a certain way which includes kicking insulation tightly or not. Some times there will be gaps, missing pieces of insulation and layers of insulation especially on tapered systems. The tapered systems will also expand the soft path of travel considerably and what seems to be a ridiculous amount of length and space. We cover that more in Perpendicular and Parallel Strategies.

In case you have never seen water drain off of one piece of insulation onto another, your not alone. Matter of fact no one really see's what goes on inside the roof. But water does fall off the edge of insulation down to lower layers and levels of the roof. Before we go on, we know that the membrane is the actual roof, but the insulation is the R-factor part of the roof. Like a hard boiled egg. You have a shell, white yolk and yellow yolk but still only one egg. Below is a nice picture of styrofoam insulation. Its very common and considered to be water proof. Again, just because material is water proof, it can still become water logged and be just as absorbent and heavy as if it were made from paper.

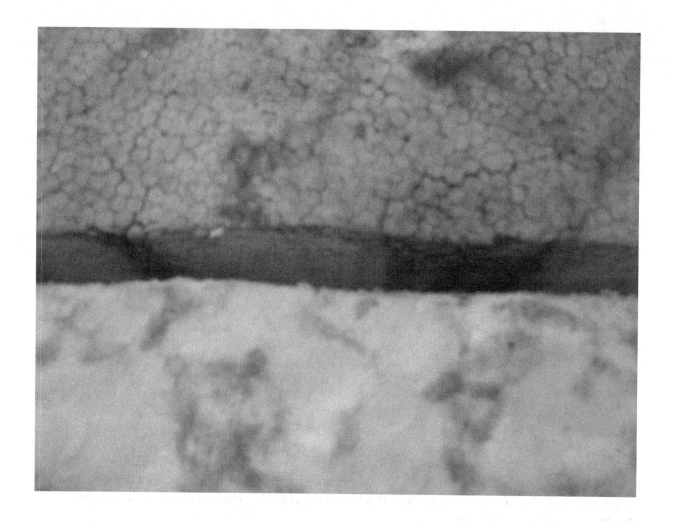

Our final full example is the Zero path of travel. Might as well get a glass of water and just pour it our on the floor at a drip a second. It is simply a path of water that drips straight through a roof structure with making a minimal amount of contact. Contact that is made by water/moisture will be by a unit/penetration or missing cap, any and all inner non-roof related problems.

Residuals from chapter 6

The path of travel is the length of water between the entry point and exit point within the roof.

There are three paths of travel to be concerned with.

Hard Path: The hard path is associated with the decking only.

Soft Path: The soft path is associated with insulation, vapor barriers and fire rating material.

Zero Path: The zero path is not associated with the roof as this path of travel makes no contact with the roof structure, only non-roof related items.

If the laps of the decking as sealed together tightly water will travel on greater distances making the hard path very extensive.

If the decking is on a slope and laps point down hill, the path of travel will always be extensive.

Loose fitting laps always shorten the path of travel.

Weld holes/blow holes always shorten the hard path of travel.

The Soft path of travel is usually short however, because of construction practices if the insulation is kicked extremely tight during installation of the insulation and the deck is sloped, the soft path of water can be extensive as well depending on the absorption rate of the insulation.

The soft path of travel can also be extended even further yet with layers of insulation such as designs associated with tapered systems and even more so travel can be expected if there is a vapor barrier.

Developed roof leaks always have a path of travel.

Chapter 7

Reservoirs

In the photo above we have what is known as a reservoir. In reality, there maybe many reservoirs scattered across a roof at any given time, depending on circumstances they may or may not actively feed a roof leak at a visible level. One of the most important parts of any roof leak is the reservoir. All legitimate roof leaks have at least one small or many reservoirs as it is a necessary and functional part of a roof leak.

Some may argue that a reservoir is the same as the path of travel because they can by sharing the same exact space to be one in the same. Not correct. The path of travel is essentially the length and direction of water within the system at deck level and a reservoir fuels the activity, regulates the activity rate of a roof leak and can exist almost anywhere you have vapor barriers, decking or insulation/multiple roof membranes.

There are four types of reservoirs that you will be dealing with on a regular basis. Reservoirs can hold a few drops, or up to hundreds of gallons of water. They can also be a couple of inches in length to hundreds of feet long. Reservoirs can double or triple the weight of the roof over time and can become a serious safety issue if not addressed within a reasonable amount of time. What is a reasonable amount of time? How long does it really take to rot a building from top to bottom?

Depending on the materials, ten years? Maybe 100 years? A slate roof being manufactured from slate will last on average 300 years. Does this mean they will not get a roof related problem that causes long term damage? Absolutely not. Its is very rarely a large disaster that destroys a building more than a small roof leak that goes unchecked or unattended for a long period of time that can destroy a historic or very productive place of business for ever.

Hard Reservoir

Soft Reservoir

Dead Reservoir

Vertical Reservoir

First, the Hard Reservoir. This type of reservoir lies directly within the flutes of metal decking. Hard reservoirs are also defined as water physically laying on decking whether it is wood, metal or concrete that is not draining. If water is found to be lying any time on top of any of these types of decking, you have a hard reservoir.

Hard reservoirs happen on all types of decking, except for sloped decked, and the resin and spaghetti type decking.

Reservoirs for the most part hard, soft even dead and vertical are rarely ever seen by the naked eye unless the roof is being torn off. You may not be able to see them often but they are there and can be identified usually after the fact. Residual drainage is good evidence of a hard reservoir.

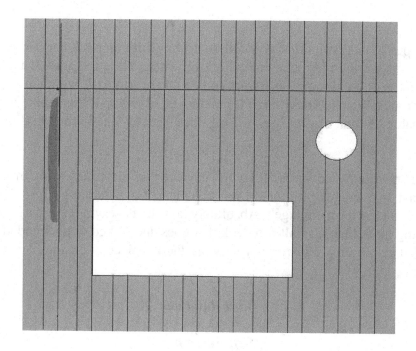

Metal decking can lie so tightly over a lap that the water will not be able to pass through, or go in between the lap and drain out as mentioned before. This creates the most commonly seen hard reservoir like in illustration 1d. Again, this water within the system is always a reservoir until the water physically begins to drain out. The reservoir becomes part of the path of travel that ends at an exit point. The reservoir feeds the roof leak for long or short amounts of time, and the path of travel decides where the activity will appear.

Reservoirs can be created by a previous tear off that has left gravel and debris within the flutes of the decking, essentially damming up the water, trapping it inside. This may cause water to overflow to corresponding flutes like in illustration 2d.

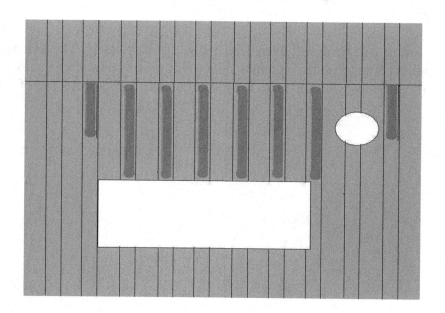

Anytime you have water just lying on any type of decking and it is not draining in anyway, you have a Dead Reservoir.

The second and most dangerous type of reservoir that is will seen is the Dead reservoir. A Dead reservoir is stagnant water within the roof system at the deck level that over time causes heavy oxidation or rusting to the deck. When the bottom side of the decking is painted over, it can be very difficult to identify from below. There by someone, maybe you or a crew member has a chance to fall through, will little to no warning.

Picture above shows a now dried out and dead reservoir. Notice how the sheet metal fasteners have been sealed by oxidization.

Two identified Dead reservoirs in the photo above. These two Dead reservoirs were never active. We found them by accident. Sooner they are discovered, the better.

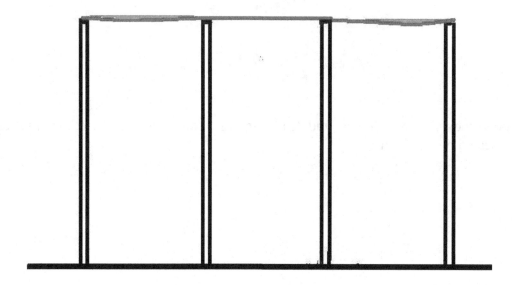

Sagging decking often produces Dead reservoirs as in the illustration above. This is why we are careful not to lay heavy items on the roof to prevent this type of damage. When water is added, we could have substantial reservoirs that may not dry or evaporate quickly creating a dangerous scenario.

The third type of reservoir is the Soft Reservoir. If you have ever helped tear off an old fibered type board insulated roof with scoop shovels, you have probably witnessed how heavy a small scoop full of this wet insulation can weigh.

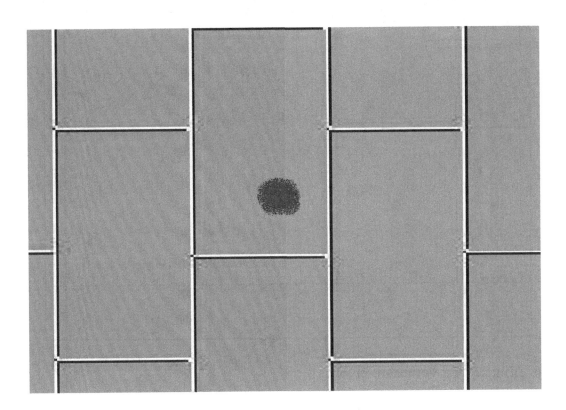

Soft reservoirs is simply wet insulation. In my drawing above we are demonstrating a fiberboard type material with a single wet area. This small are can hold a lot of water if left unchecked. When you conduct a Trough Search, this is what you will be looking for, but you won't be able to see it.

The fourth and final reservoir you will run into every now and then is the Vertical Reservoir.

Vertical reservoirs, water lying within wall flashings or along penetrations, as water is trapped within the layers of material. Vertical reservoirs usually hold a small amount of water and never become active. Just about every roof has one Vertical reservoir of some type. This is simply another way of saying that we have water trapped within pockets of wall flashings or the walls of penetrations.

We have always cut them out or drained them and never messed with them again. Usually, they just look bad but never really do any real damage.

The longer it takes to fill a reservoir, the longer the wait for the roof leak to become active, and the longer it takes to stop the unwanted activity. Reservoirs are the main cause of residual drainage.

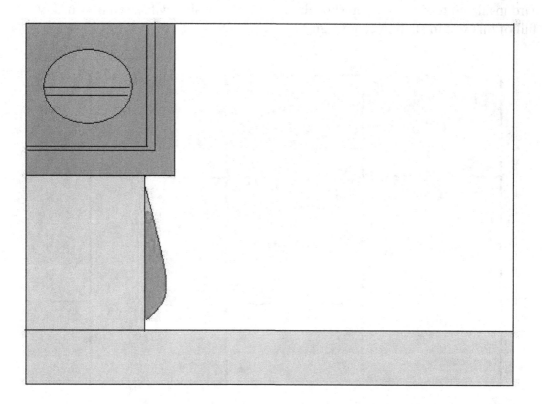

Above an example of a Vertical reservoir.

Residuals from chapter 7

There are four types of reservoirs.

A Hard reservoir is water lying on, or water collecting over any type of decking.

Hard Reservoirs will not be found with the resin spaghetti type decking.

A Soft Reservoir is water collected and stored within different types of wood or paper based insulation board type accessories.

Reservoirs can slow the start of a roof leak and drag out the time of residual drainage at the end of the activity.

Dead Reservoirs are usually hidden and can be very dangerous or even fatal to unwitting repairmen or visitors on the roof.

Vertical Reservoirs are non-active pockets of water usually associated with wall flashings and cured/uncured flashings.

Chapter 8

Entry Points

The final and most positive indicator/factor that you have a legitimate roof leak is the entry point. An Entry point can be a cut, hole, split, tear, etc., in the roof membrane. Question will be after an entry point has been discovered, is this the only one? In the photo above we have a jagged 7 inch rip in 0.045 EPDM membrane. This leak had been active for twelve years.

This identifying marker we call an entry point can exist on all types of roofs regardless of the material its manufactured out of, in one form or another. This final identifier makes the roof leak 100% legitimate and absolutely not related to other sources. You must be able to identify all types of entry points, many entry points will look similar, but like snowflakes they are all unique to the roof in question.

Roof maintenance or HVAC people have been known to stumble upon an entry point or two. If you do get a call where you have to repair something found by another person other than a roofer, you should search the entire area. You may look foolish if you patch one entry point and missed thirty others. Even more foolish yet, if that smooth move caused thousands of dollars of damage, after you told them everything was good to go.

Sharp Objects such as dropped knives, screwdrivers, access doors to HVAC units. Fireworks, broken bottles, bullets, rocks/ballast that are broken and sharp, are waiting with sharp edges to be stepped on. Any innocent looking object can easily cut through the membrane by a single person while innocently making a single step onto the roof.

Been witness to two guys sharing a pair of scissors as they were throwing the scissors back and forth from one end of the roof to the other. A couple of times they hit the roof and bounced around a little. Immediately I went over and inspected the roof. There were no cuts, slices or entry points at all. Just a couple of scuff marks on the surface.

Three years later, at the same location I had to go back out for some roof leaks. Guess what? The holes I found were exactly where the scissors were bouncing around on the roof surface. Even when you drop something inert on the surface of the roof, think about how much expansion and contraction that roof goes through every single moment of the day.

In the picture above, we have a large entry point done while the roof was being installed. Entry point was found under the paver. Can't explain it, almost looks intentionally cut out.

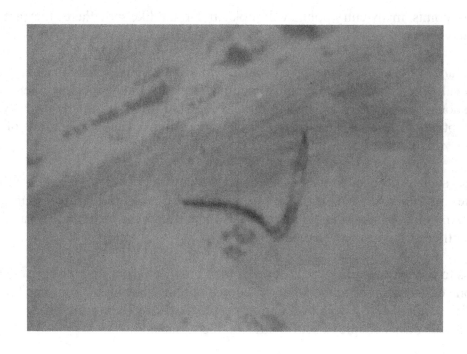

Above we have the most common Entry point, known for its shape the V-cut. V-cut sizes may vary from microscopic to several feet or more across.

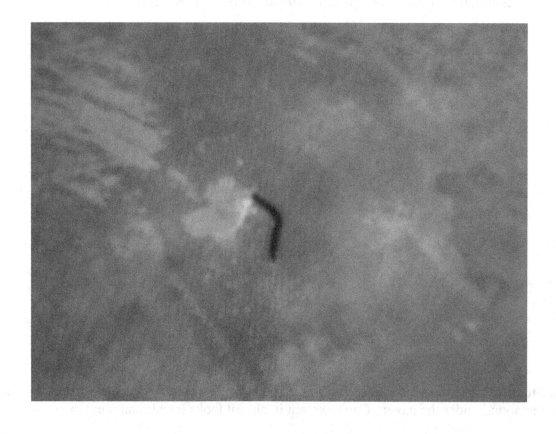

The picture above has what most do not see. This is an Entry point caused by a pipe. Apparently, this person walked around jabbing a metal pipe into the roof. He was visiting from out of state doing one single job on the roof. Below, V-cut, over a plate.

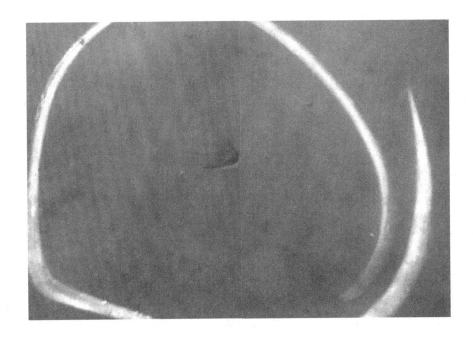

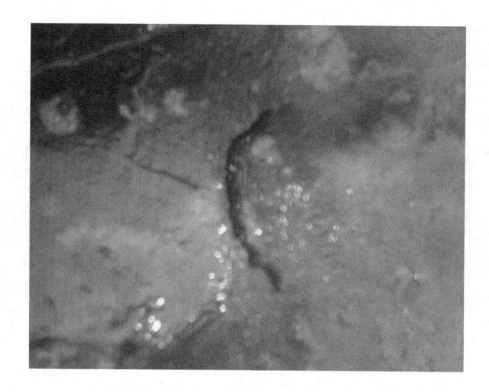

In the picture above cured flashing with entry point that continued through roof membrane. We could not identify it until we removed the mud off the top of the membrane. Picture below shows what one fallen tree can do to a single ply rubber roof. This one tree falling over on this roof made about 75 entry points.

Most entry points, will develop and open up when the roof losses oils, and natural lubricants that allow the roof to expand and contract. Dropping a one half inch by two-foot long metal pipe on the roof, probably would not make a cut in the membrane. Rest assured, there will be an entry point present one day caused by natural expansion/contraction of the membrane.

When any large/small but heavy object falls hard enough on membrane, it pushes out the oils microscopically in whatever the shape of the object that makes contact with the surface. With expansion and contraction an entry point will develop. This of course takes years.

And if you look across the surface of the roof you will see a rough texture kind of like indents. We call these indents, "Divots." Divots are usually harmless and can easily be confused with very entry points. They are simply factory made small imperfections made by tiny molecules of oxygen at the factory only on the surface of the membrane.

Important note, V-cuts are not caused by birds.

The most difficult to track entry point on a roof is the fine line cuts. These cuts can be so fine that you have to spread the rubber apart with you fingers to actually see them. This is why you must be "Touchy Feely," on all roof surfaces.

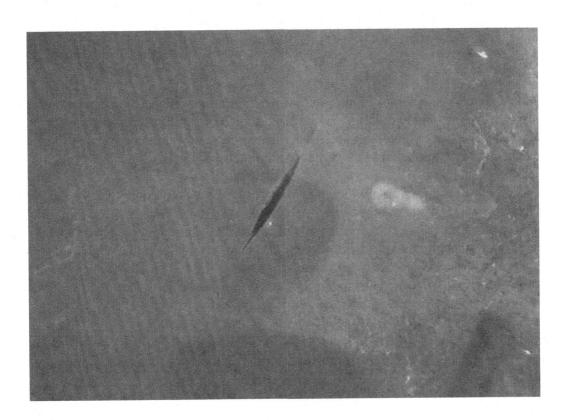

If the membrane is over twenty to twenty five years old and its only, .045 mil., thick, long term evaporation can create Micro-entry points. For instance in the next picture we have a smooth .045 mil., roof that is over twenty-two years old. Notice how many Micro-entry points have been identified. We replaced the sheet after finding over 350, mini entry points. We have a macro-amount of micro-entry points.

Entry points can produce complex or simple roof leak scenarios such as, one entry point can produce 15 exit points. Alternatively, you can have fifteen entry points that produce only one exit point. Regardless of exit/entry points these micro-entry points are very difficult to spot, and are to be expected with roofs that have well exceeded their life cycle.

It really says a lot for the roofing producing companies that have a product that is so reliable that it exceeds its life cycle two and three times. As one would expect, fully adhered and reinforced membrane type applications do not produce V-cuts as easy as smooth, loosely laid EPDM. If there is a tear in the membrane of a reinforced EPDM roof, it may resemble a V-cut just because of the direction. To create a V-cut or tear on a reinforced EPDM, it would have to be extreme and on purpose. Usually you will discover pinholes, punctures or tears. You will rarely ever see damage from stretching, tearing or expansive entry points on reinforced EPDM.

Often repair people go up on the roof and are satisfied with finding one entry point. Do not stop until you have searched out every square inch of your search areas because it's so easy to miss the smallest Entry points.

Once in a while, you will find a glue all lap type of EPDM roof with an opening in the lap. That too, is an entry point. Below a circular cut over a plate, EPDM roof.

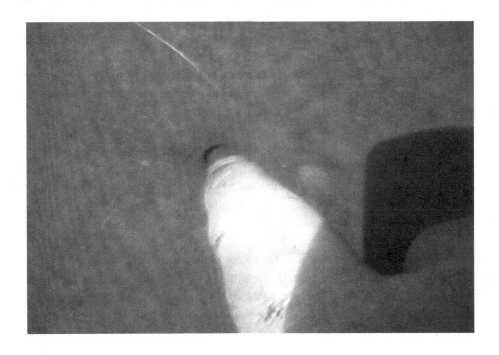

Something most people do not realize is that it's important what time of year that the entry point was made. Depending on what time of year will decide its exposure and actual size of visibility to the naked eye.

For example, if we have a roof and its summer time, also in the hottest part of the afternoon and we slice the membrane with a razor knife and left it to the elements. When we come back to that same entry point/slice in the wintertime, what do you think has happened to the entry point? Will it be larger, or smaller?

Consider this, when the membrane gets cold during the wintertime, the membrane will contract. When the membrane contracts, the entry point will be larger as the membrane will pull from all directions equally, thereby opening the entry point wider, making it more visible to the naked eye. This entry point will be easy to see, solve and fix in the winter, compared to summer.

What if the same piece of roof has an entry point made around wintertime and we left it alone until summer? Would it be easier to see?

We know that membrane like all material expands in warmer temperatures. If there is an excess of material and warm conditions an entry point may be more difficult to identify because the membrane would enclose itself.

Because of this circumstance, some entry points are very difficult to identify with the naked eye. This is why we must be Touchy feely when it comes to roof membrane while searching for an entry point. Touchy feely means we have to physically touch the material, spread is apart if possible and try to find the entry point especially when there is an excess of material.

Temperature changes can affect membrane anytime through out the year or day. If the temperature travels twenty degrees one way or another, this can open or close these entry points out of view. These entry points will also open up as the sun goes down and the material and temperature cool down and contract. Its gradual and you need a time-lapse camera to see the slight movement actually happen. They will not open and close completely by any means, but they do react to these temperature changes and these changes can make the entry point easier, or more difficult to identify to the naked eye.

This might explain when we have been up on a roof, and found absolutely no entry points, but later it leaked again in the exact location, and upon entering the roof again, you find an entry point. Where did that come from? Fact of the matter is, it was there the whole time but hid in plain sight. When an entry point is not defined enough or large enough to be identified with the naked eye, your task is very difficult.

Fully adhered roof systems will have very little to no expansion and contraction but for the rest of them, even built-up roofs will have a certain amount of expansion or contraction that may regulate and/or affect the way a roof leak behaves, and may hide identifying factors, making it invisible to the naked eye. Surprisingly once in a while, you will probably run into an entry point that has never taken in any water.

If there is an overhead type canopy at a certain area of a roof like ventilation ductwork, if the entry point location is up out of the valley or low-lying areas, it may never have the opportunity to take in water as it may be shielded from the weather. Or, the entry point may be up on a peak and there has never been enough water to travel through to lead anyone to it before. Therefore it grows unchecked until a really big weather event exposes everything, even the ten year roof leaks.

Sometimes it really is up to luck, chance or circumstance whether or not a roof leak not only exists, but also luck that it is active enough to be tracked back to an entry point. This is the main reason we always check over the roof even if it is a quick walk through to look for the possibility of unidentified entry points that may be connected in some way.

An entry point can be anywhere on a roof. Do not forget to take pictures of all entry points. Our customers favorite part of the visit was when we showed them pictures of the roof related problem, entry point and repair. Its very powerful and shows you are doing your job. There will always be the possibility that the repair that you make is not the right one to stop the leak you are search for. As long as you photograph the progress with positive and constructive work, it is not considered a failure, or a loss column situation. Its only the natural order of things. As you continue on, your success rate will continue on higher and you will become more confident as this information one day will become old fashion.

A picture of an entry point is a picture of success.

Residuals from chapter 8

An entry point is an opening or openings in the roof membrane that allows water into the roof system and into the building causing countless dollars in damages and loss of R-factor which results in even more dollars lost.

An entry point can vary in size from micro to macro and mini to large. From a centimeter or an eight of an inch in diameter up to hundreds of feet/meters.

Micro entry points are the most difficult to identify.

Macro entry points are the easiest to identify.

Entry points are usually identified in the field as; cuts, holes, splits, tears, V-shaped cuts.

One entry point can produce multiple roof leaks/exit points, many entry points may produce only one roof leak/exit point.

The most commonly seen entry point is the V-cut.

Its almost impossible to make a V-cut on a reinforced membrane type roof.

Laps in the field or flashings that have come apart are also considered entry points because they allow water into the system through the roof membrane that has been permanently joined with adhesives.

Termination type bar, bib-flashings and any other metal device that seals an edge are not considered roof related entry points.

95% of all entry points are man made.

Naturally occurring entry points include, weather, animal and cause 5% of all entry points.

Depending on circumstances, some entry points are almost impossible to identify with the naked eye.

Temperature and season can determine the actual visible size of an entry point.

Not all entry points produce regularly active roof leaks.

Chapter 9

Dual Point Positioning

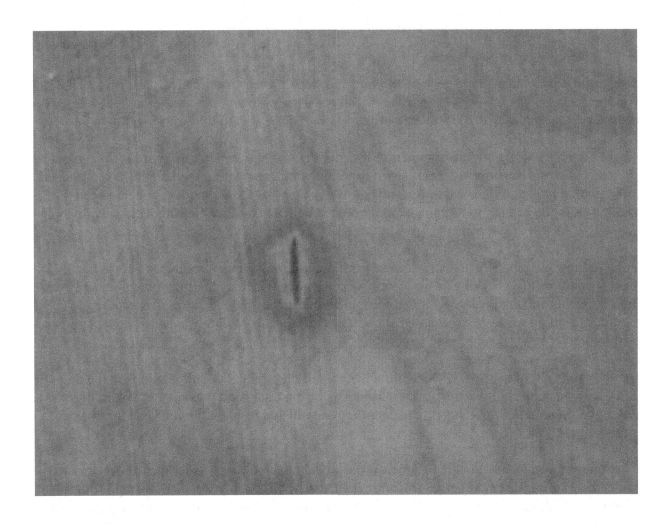

We discovered this entry point two hundred and sixty feet away from the exit point. We would not have found it if it were not for Dual Point Positioning. Stepping off a relatively small area is not a problem most of the time but it can become confusing and even more so are large spaces with long lengths.

Dual point positioning means exactly what it says. There are two points we are concerned about, the exit point and entry point. Dual meaning two, and positioning yourself over the leak area and identifying the exact exit point on the surface of the roof by utilizing measurements you acquire from inside the building itself. Without an accurate measurement that is transferred to the roof, finding the entry point can be very difficult.

Securing good measurements can result in a definite find or a good starting point. What if we could prove the entry point found directly measures up to the exit point? Good news as we can be more sure of our task. That's what this is all about, certainty.

MESUREMENTS WILL ALWAYS BE BASED ON NORTH/SOUTH EAST/WEST

Dual point positioning should be used as your first step on every roof related problem to help you focus, and save time. Developed specifically to narrow down or increase the field where necessary, this application if completed properly can reduce wasted time and frustration.

Always double check your measurements, and make new measurements every time you go out, even if it's for the same repeat leak. There is nothing more frustrating then having a roof related problem that refuses to die, and to find several visits later that the wrong location had been secured from the beginning. Again, even if you go back out on the same roof leak call, always get new or fresh measurements to prevent this situation from occurring.

To save time and money you really need to get a precise measurement of the actual roof leak at an exit point from the decking as we went over in chapter 5. Most repair people utilize only two measurements and that's okay for small jobs, but when an absolute location needs to be recorded, nothing works better than Dual point positioning. We will always utilize Dual point positioning for repeat leak calls or larger jobs.

Before you begin measuring, consider the thickness of the walls. For starters, look at the door jams that you entered into at any given building. The building itself can have a foot or more of block and brick, and do not forget to account for drywall and insulation which can throw your measurements off.

Its strongly recommend you utilize a measuring wheel of some type. Laser measuring devices can be helpful if utilized properly. Unfortunately, many will simply walk off or step off the area. If you do decide to chance strides/steps to measure off the leak in relation to some landmark or outer walls, be careful. Make sure the strides you take are consistent on the ground level as on the roof, and counted properly.

The most common mistake while doing this is simply miscounting. One-step is not enough to throw you off completely, that is if you do not add more mistakes to the formula. The larger the roof, the bigger the mistakes with our measurements can be.

Some roofs are very long in length and width making the possibilities of more mistaken measurements almost inevitable, use a measuring wheel on the large jobs when possible is the key to accuracy. One building I know of is over a mile long. How can we match up the upper and lower locations properly, and confirm that as close as possible using math? There is a simple formula behind it.

$$10 \;\; \frac{10}{10} \;\; 10$$

If you hate fractions do not fret, these are not fractions. Notice the numbers ten over ten by ten by ten above? That's not a fraction that's a location. This is a general or basic measurement of a building. The parallel line in the middle of the equation shows us the direction of our decking. These numbers are always based on true north.

First, let's talk about breaking the building up. In illustration we have a large building with an attached addition. If there are no roof related problems within this additional area and the decking does not connect through the wall, ignore this and all other separated additional areas.

This negative process can also be eliminated. Don't site see.

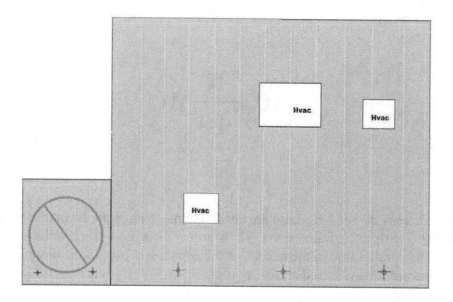

We have a roof leak at the red dot in the lower left hand corner in the larger part of the building. We have identified all four walls and our true north location. We know where the very outer edge of our building is located.

Measure these outer wall locations without trying to go around obstructions and equipment. Sometimes we have to walk out in the middle of isle ways to get a good measurement. This is something you and your helper can work out.

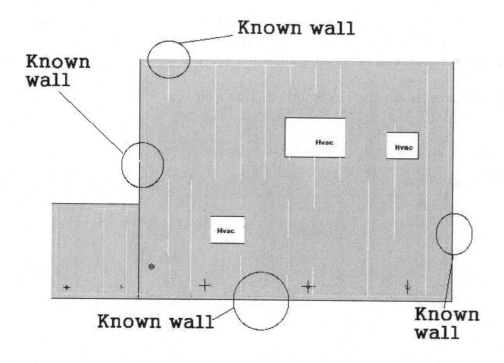

We will say that our section of building in our illustration is 40 meters by 40 meters

square (not to scale). Our exit point is 3 meters from the south wall and 37 meters
from the north wall.

In addition, our exit point is 1 step from the west wall and 39 steps from the east wall. How
would you write it? Remember our decking runs from north to south. It should look like the
equation on the next page.

$$37$$
$$1 \mid 39$$
$$3$$

Now what happens? This is the easy part. With your measurements, you will head up on the
roof and begin laying out your search area.

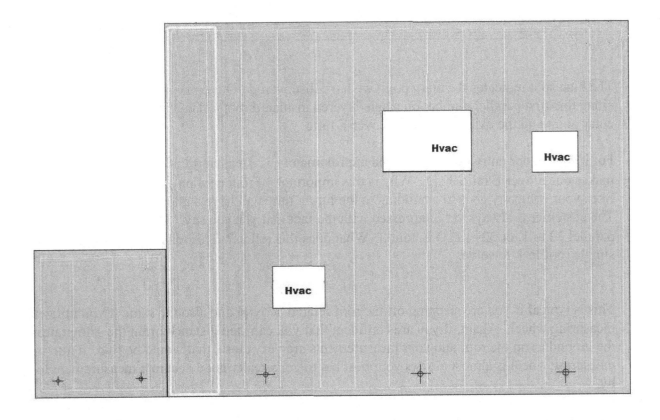

Search grids in yellow are covered in Chapter 11, this example is just to give you a sense of the
importance and value of the actual application. Remember our decking runs from north to south.

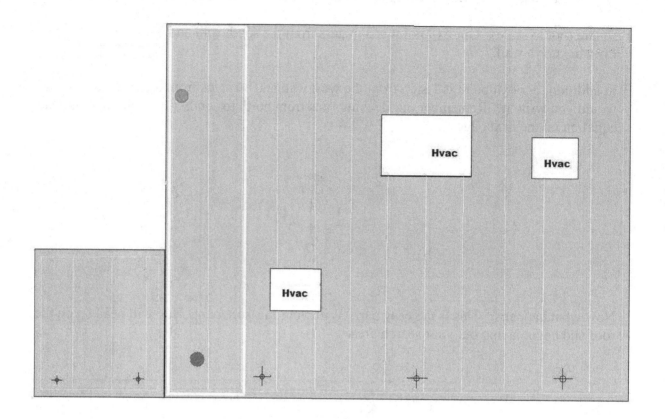

The blue spot indicates the entry point we have discovered. Our entry point will usually fall along this first parallel number on single layered insulated roofs. The difference between the entry point and the exit point is our E over E ratio.

For instance, our entry point was found approximately 32 steps north of our exit point. This makes our E over E ratio 32 | 1. Why is this important? From now on any time you or someone from your company goes to a building in the future they will have a good idea of what to expect. The customer is always very impressed with the fact that you can say, "Our E over E ratio is a parallel 32 to 1, or 32 | 1 E.O.E. ratio." What does this tell us? This tells us that it was a pretty simple roof leak to solve.

This is typical if you are stepping off the roof related activity and also the same if you utilize a measuring wheel. Again, if you are confident that you can step distance off at the same rate on the ground as on the roof and your measurements are very close, that would be find. Truth is, measuring wheel is almost always your best bet to get a really good accurate measurement to go by.

Now that you have a basic understanding of what is expected for an accurate account of your roof related problem lets make it more realistic. Let us look at is as you would on the job. Let us look at the actual roof from our illustration.

This is a reinforced rubber membrane roof above. The super imposed red spot is our actual leak location. Below is the actual exit point seen from inside the building. The yellow lines show our perpendicular and parallel lines.

Because the building was not that large in scale we walked it off, and this was not a repeat leak, and there was no gravel to hamper our search efforts.

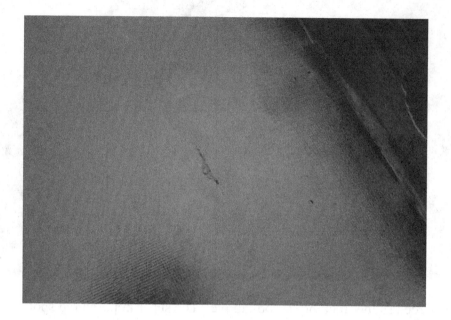

After utilizing dual point positioning we were able to easily find the entry point in this smooth re-enforced EPDM roof.

Above the actual tear in the membrane. Below is our temporary repair.

We were forced to make a temp until a drier day.

Just because you can make a repair in between raindrops, humidity and dew point may prevent a more permanent repair. How do we confirm that we have a bulls eye? We will take measurements from the entry point on the roof and compare them to the exit point measurement. That gets us as close as possible, that doesn't guarantee that we didn't miss something small. Detail, detail and more detail.

The first set of numbers below on the right is the location of our entry point. Set on the left shows our measurement of the exit point.

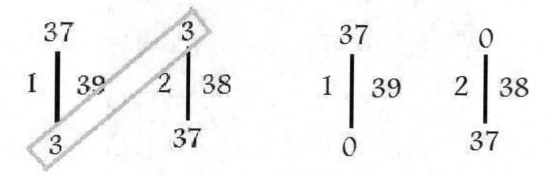

Deduct your bottom E (3) number from your top E (3) number you end up with zero.

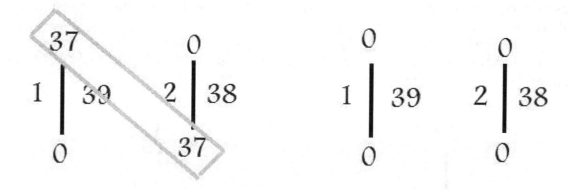

Now deduct your top E of 37 from your bottom E of 37 and you also have zero.
Taking your 1 from 2 and you have 1. Finally, you take 38 from 39 and you have 1, this is a solution of 1:1. Easily fixed and confirmed.

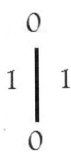

There is a marginal level of accuracy and on the other hand, because of circumstances relating to the insulation and slope that dictate the closeness of the entry point to the exit point. Getting close is a big deal especially when there is nothing else to be found.

Dual point position is not anything new, we all do it to begin our investigation, however to be more accurate we, our helper and ourselves take measurements, measure it off and compare the two to ensure that we at least close. When the two match up closely enough, we begin our search with the proper search grid.

Rather than running up on the roof and patching the first and only thing discovered, take the time to collect the right measurements below, write them down in a way that they can be understood and read back on the roof. It really is worth the effort and don't forget to utilize a measuring wheel for a more accurate location to begin your search.

Take advantage of it when you can.

Residuals from chapter 9

Dual Point Positioning is utilized to confirm the location of an exit point in relation to the entry point.

Dual Point Positioning are always based on compass measurements.

Always write down all measurements taken inside the building at the Exit point(s).

Always utilize a measuring wheel when attempting Dual point positioning.

Dual point positioning is to be completed by supervisor and helper and is to be compared for better accuracy.

Smaller jobs do not require Dual point positioning.

Dual point positioning is to be utilized on all repeat or return leak calls.

Dual point positioning can also be achieved with a laser-measuring device.

Chapter 10

Perpendicular and Parallel Strategies

Perpendicular and Parallel Strategies is utilizing your exit point measurements for more predictable and complete variables relating to the decking, insulation and directional possibilities as to the natural diversionary information required to successfully locate a particular roof leak.

In other words, securing a definite area to begin our search, we have to make sure that we cover enough area to locate the problem without going over board with our time. After collecting measurements from our exit point(s), we can mark out the search area.

You can mark your search area with chalk, and do not over mark the roof. Make marks on outside lines, mark the direction of the deck and mark the location of the exit point found down stairs to the top surface of the membrane. Do not forget to mark true north with an arrow with an N under it. Try to use temporary chalk, like kids play chalk.

This information once written on the roof will keep you aware of the direction and location as it relates to downstairs. Remember when down stairs, collect information such as, compass locations, discovering the levelness of the decking. Finally, activity rate, if leak is active when you arrive on site or not.

Activity rate is when you measure the amount of water dripping from an exit point during a one-minute interval. Any measuring cup will do, but a measuring flask looks more professional. Of course, after making a repair, you will complete an additional activity rate check to confirm, more or less activity if attempted during a rain event. Note: A steady and constant rain even is one certain way to get complete and accurate possible changing rate amounts from an active roof leak. If you take a measurement during a heavy rain event, then later when the rain has either slowed down or stopped, the rate will automatically be different and you will not have useful information as to pertaining to effectiveness of your investigation.

A search grid is a wonderful fail safe item that makes roof leaks less likely to be left behind or over looked. Many times, just by accident we would find an entry point much further away than we ever imagined. There was one commonality, they would almost always stay within the say part of the decking which we have identified already as our path of travel. Always in the same channel, flute of decking. Water you see, rarely ever crosses over the top rib of decking. It can and will if given the opportunity.

If you have dented-in decking that is already low-lying and there is debris within the flutes of decking, water can and will travel over not only one or two ribs but sometimes many. Because of the variables of the loosely laid decking, and decking that is so tightly put together that water can weep, or travel between the laps, consideration has to be applied in a realistic and automatic way to save time.

You would not want to search a 5000 square foot building, when the decking could be loosely laid and the entry point will probably be over or near a couple of sheets of decking as by average. But how do we know this? A lot has to do with history. If you know the building has a history of problematic roof leaks, you must increase you search grid. If the roof has multiple layers of insulation, or even a vapor barrier, you must increase the search grid as well. All of this adds either weight to the decking which causes water to carry further away. Also, the vapor barriers and fire rating materials cause additional travel sideways in the form of a maze.

To prevent over stepping or under stepping our efforts, we first much look at the what is required.

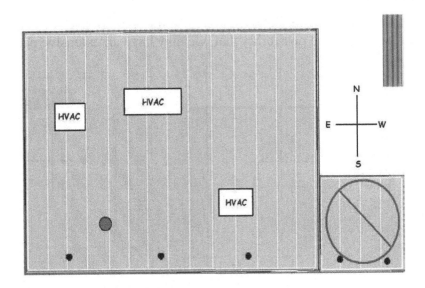

Our fictitious roof above, in the illustration marked in red our exit point is south of and between two HVAC units. Our building is 28' by 34' feet. In these examples exit points are presented in red, yellow represents entry points.

Many repair people will create a small grid and focus in on a small search area. Notice in the illustration below, we have an example of metal decking above our compass setting. Decking is 8 foot in length.

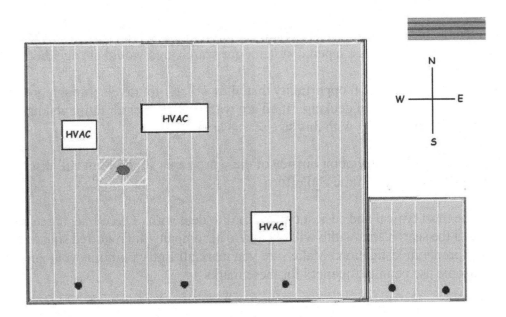

Many repair people will make the mistake of searching just barely eight or ten feet around the exit point or actual leak area. Notice the direction of the decking? At the bottom of the roof are drains which indicates the roof slopes north to south.

Chances of securing an entry point are about 15%. At a minimum these particularly small search areas do not take into account the possibility that, we may have an extensive path of travel.

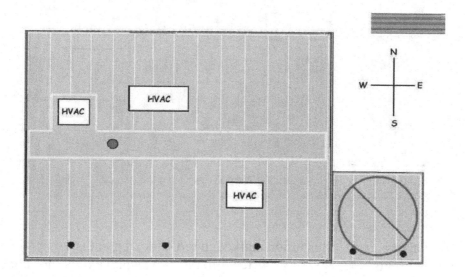

Above in our illustration, is what the minimum search area should look like for any roof at a minimum. The search area always runs parallel with the direction of the decking. The width of our minimum search area is 20' feet on center. In other words from the very exit point center mark, we go 10' feet in both sides of the center of the red and the entire length of the decking from end to end of the building.

We always add units/penetrations that are relatively close to our search area. If building/roof was built with a slope or there is a tapered system, our search area would change dramatically.

The reasoning for this is based on opportunity that allows water to travels through one layer of membrane, across insulation and decking. If all are within a 1:1 over all ratio, you have a 98% chance of finding the entry point with this size search area.

It's not unusual to find the Entry point outside of the search area slightly but still discovered at or about that acceptable margin of time and effort.

Again, this is the most typical and easiest type of roof to deal with. Of course, it gets more complicated, and the search area width will expand to accompany the required square footage for a complete and proper investigation. Make sure you mark all Entry points as you come upon them. Some people use pennies, quarters for these marks.

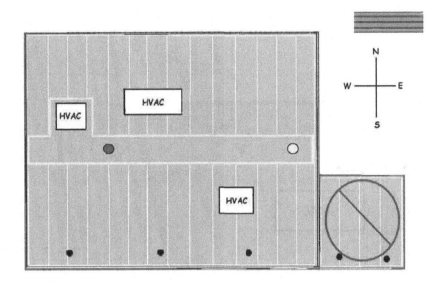

In illustration above, we have the proper standard search area for the proper type of roof. Did we miss the entry point with our original and typical search area? Yes, we did miss it, completely. This would have been a trip out to the customer with no real results. This is what often creates return or repeat roof leak calls.

What if our decking was running from north to south? Would it make a difference in the length or width of our search area? The answer is no.

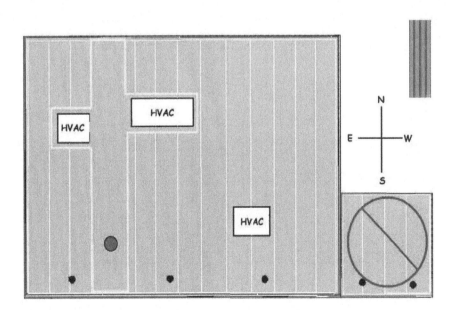

There is still one layer of roof, insulation with medium to high sloped metal decking. We included additional units into the investigation due to their close proximity to our search area.

Level 1:1

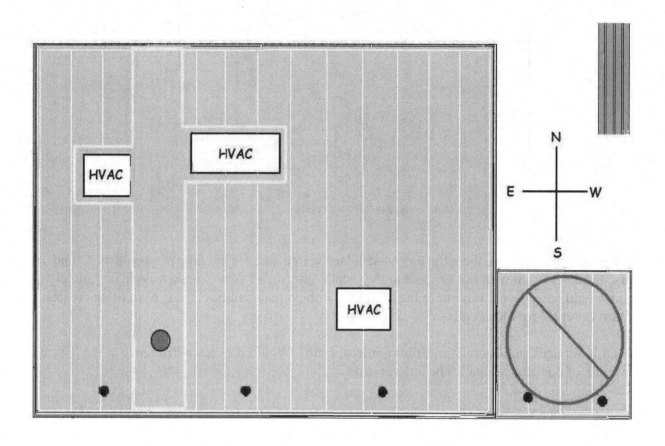

Next Level Up-2:1

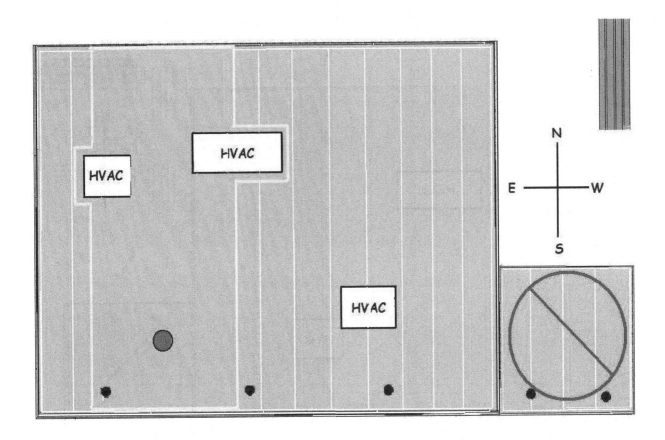

Illustration above is the size search area if, roof is on a medium slope or two or more layers of insulation, or if the O.A.R., is 2:1. This also increases our search area to 30' feet wide. Not on center, ten feet below our exit point location, twenty feet above.

We added to the size of our search area, but not downhill or below our entry point. Remember that water runs down hill, most of the time. If there is blockage at a low lying area within the system, water can fill up at an area and back flow slightly up hill. This of course is an illusion. Water does not run up hill, but can back flow if we have sunken decking or insulation that is warped or damaged in a way to allow water to flow in the opposite direction. This is called Ramping Up.

Next Level Up-3:1

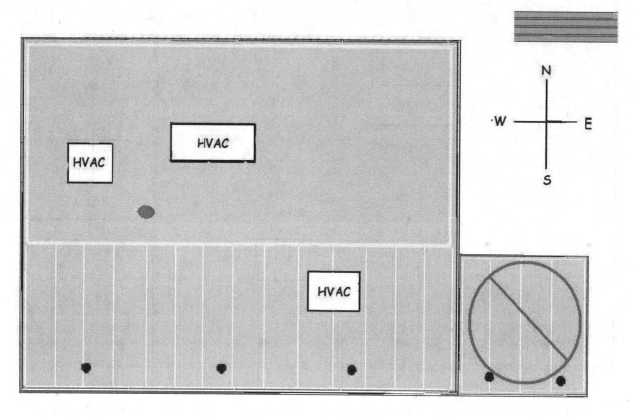

In the illustration above, we have the 3:1 O.A.R., search area. This is specifically for, a two layered roof or multiple layers of insulation, and low to medium slope. Our minimum search area will be 40 feet wide on center. Since we are on a sloped roof or tapered insulation, we will go ten feet below, and thirty feet above from our exit point location.

This compensates for the possibility of water piggy backing over insulation and the possibility of the path of travel being a great length. This may seem far and wide, but we know that we will find the entry point within this search area.

Next Level up 4:1

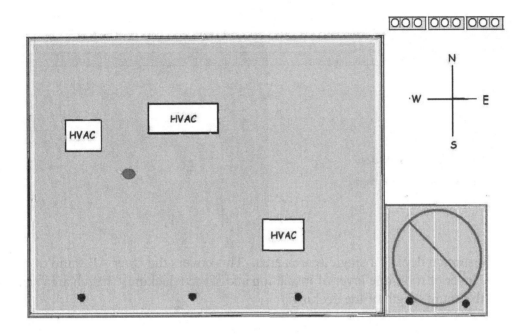

Over all ratio of 4:1 in our illustration above. This roof is completely flat or slightly sloped with multiple layers of insulation over a concrete deck. This search grid also covers multi-layered roofs of all types.

Whether you have metal deck or concrete and even wooden deck, any time you have more than one roof it is to be treated the same as multiple layers of insulation, over concrete decking you will always base you search area on the 4:1 over all ratio.

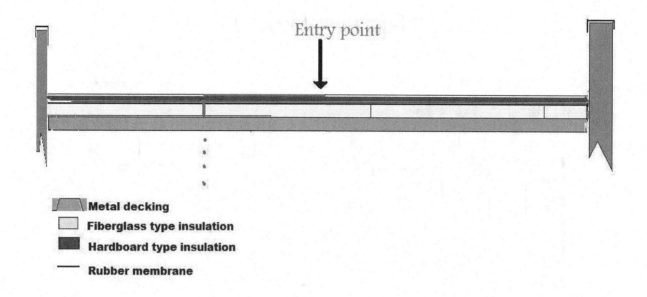

Our generic illustration depicts a single search area. This covers the Over All Ratio of 1:1. This scenario is one layer of roof, one layer of insulation and sloped decking. Search area size, 20 feet on center the entire length of the decking.

Illustration 11f.

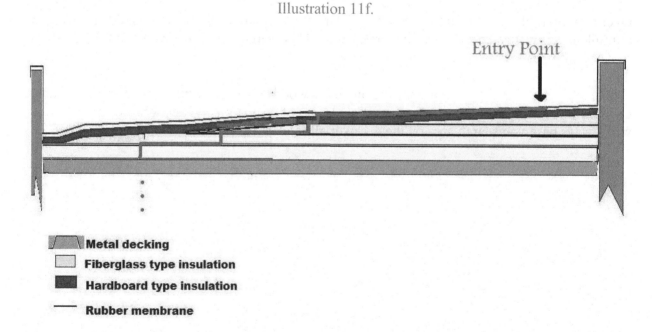

This shows us what is going on with in the parameters of a typical roof that has multiple layers of insulation. This of course is a standard tapered system. The Over all ratio here would be 2:1. Below two layers of roof and multiple layers of insulation makes our illustration, a 3:1 ratio.

Illustration 12f.

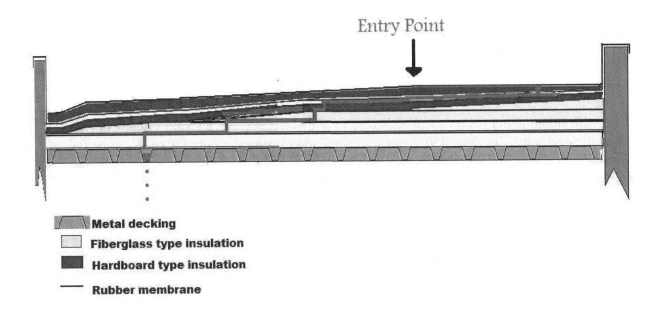

Entry Point

Metal decking
Fiberglass type insulation
Hardboard type insulation
Rubber membrane

Illustration 13f.

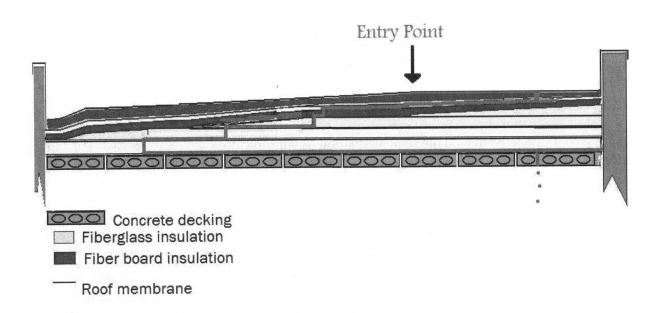

Entry Point

Concrete decking
Fiberglass insulation
Fiber board insulation
Roof membrane

The most difficult over all ratio 4:1. We have more than one roof and multiple layers of insulation. Under all of that, we have a concrete deck. This like all examples is not depicted exactly how it happens every time however, they do follow a common path similar to these types of applications.

What if you have a valley area? Think about the material and decking. Should you utilize a smaller or simple type of search area? You would search in relation to the slope, or how many possible layers of insulation and the type of decking. These examples cover what if scenarios, but are based on real life situations. The more variables, the bigger the search grid, the more to investigate.

A real life situation many don't realize is that a valley area may have a valley shape because of either the decking as its shaped to divert water to a lower central point. Often it will be the insulation that is sloped and the decking maybe flat. Always search up hill to the peak at all valley areas, but pay attention, the decking may slope the opposite direction as what is seen when looking at the tapered or sloped insulation.

These search areas are designed to capture the entry point within a specific time slot. This is so we can focus on the material, space within our required search area without wondering away from our search grid and wasting time. This also prevents us from missing something out of the ordinary that most will over look. Where others quit and fail, you will be able to draw an absolute conclusion when it comes to where to begin searching and when you should stop.

When utilizing these basic search areas that are based on the difficulty of the roof and circumstances, rest assured that you will not be missing much. Only what you over look, should be a concern. These are the bare minimum search areas and are to be utilized regardless, even if you easily find an entry point, search out the entire area.

Some repair people will stop when they find one entry point. They may make the repair and go to the next job. If they utilized the minimal search area, they may discover other possibly entry points. Get all the entry points that are related to each individual leak. If you do not, the leak will tell on you. Now that you see what is expected from the bare minimum to maximum search areas, let's talk about different types of roofs.

Built-up roofs are to be treated the same in relation to our indicators and search areas. The only difference is the type of material utilized. These same types of search areas are also true for Torch Down, Heat Weld, etc.

Another thing about our general descriptions is that I left the gravel or ballast off our examples. Moving gravel may vary due to density and the pure manpower behind the task. When it comes to moving ballast, it does affect the over all difficulty rating and should be taken into consideration when laying out your search area due to the type of roof you area dealing with.

Remember, water can move perpendicular and parallel to and from an entry point/exit point. You really have to use your imagination and imagine how water maybe flowing within the system. Could there be an extra long path of travel? Is water piggybacking? Maybe there is Spider webbing, which is a bi-product of Piggybacking. There are so many possibilities so you can never really under estimate your search grid area.

You have to look at the roof you are working on and decide which way the water could be running to and from by your measurements. That information you collect, helps fill in the dots. Your search area will be based on, the type of roof, slope of the decking/insulation, and possible path of travel.

Residuals from chapter 10

Perpendicular and parallel strategies are to be utilized on all roofs when looking for a roof related problem.

Perpendicular and Parallel Strategies take into account, insulation elements, slope of decking and the amount of roofs to create a usable and reliable search area.

When a search area falls within 10' feet of any unit or penetration, that penetration automatically becomes part of the search area.

O.A.R. 1:1 equals a single search area which is a twenty foot O.C., wide path that runs parallel with the decking from end to end of the building.

O.A.R. 2:1 equals a double search area of 30-foot wide path that runs from end to end of the decking/building.

O.A.R. 3:1 equals double the previous search area. Usually 40 foot or wider path from end to end of the decking/building.

O.A.R. 4:1 equals entire coverage of the roof and building.

Chapter 11

Trough Search

After you finish the proper search grid, the next step is to look for rough roof surfaces. We do this by looking for sunken in areas, soft or what might look like a pond without water. We call this a Trough search. A trough search has the potential to take you straight to the roof related problem very quickly. troughing is a phenomenon that happens when insulation becomes saturated due to an entry point allowing water into the roof membrane that damages and breaks down an area known as troughing.

Troughing happens when water gets into the system, breaks down, and prematurely erodes the insulation, and reducing the R-Factor. Troughing can cover an entire roof if not caught in time.

Troughing can also run in a six-inch wide swatch by 2000 feet in length on a roof of any type commercial/industrial building. Troughing is easily identified by stepping onto both soft and hard roof areas at the same location or building/roof and comparing the difference in density.

Even though most of us see it regularly, we really do not pay attention to it. A good exercise to do that will help you understand troughing, is to go where there was once a known active leak. Look where the repair was made, look for the troughing. You may come across many troughed areas that have been repaired previously. The water that is in the system will eventually dissipate however, the damage is done. Unless you replace the insulation, it will always be a troughed area.

Dry Troughing above is caused by the weight of water or heavy items laying on the roof surface over a long period of time.

Troughing is a footprint left behind. What type of activity made the Troughed area is the important thing to figure out, as soon as possible. Usually if you feel with your feet and look closely, you may be able to recognize these naturally occurring processes. Troughing never appears on walls.

Another cause of wide spread dry troughing is rubber membrane roofs that have been re-skinned. Typically, the insulation is flipped over and recycled. This process makes conducting a trough search very difficult for repair people.

If you find a roof that has been re-skinned, be careful! You can get false positives everywhere. This can make conducting a trough searching almost impossible. If you get into that extreme situation, you may have to resort to Surgical Intervention. We will cover that later.

A tiny hole or split anywhere along or within this Troughed area could be causing a problem. If you run into this type of situation and the leak is active, move the water and check in and around the edge of the puddles.

If during your visit, the leak is not active, check around the outside parameters of the troughing. Chances are good, the entry point will be active if underwater. Do not walk mindlessly through the puddles or troughed areas. The reason for that is when we walk through puddles, we soak the roof. We are less likely to be able to utilize I.T.I., covered in the next chapter.

Mechanical fasteners may appear to back out sometimes through the membrane. In the picture below you see a screw head that is the same height as the rest of the roof, but because of severe troughing, the insulation has broken down making the screw appear as if it's backing out. In reality, it has not moved, only the insulation.

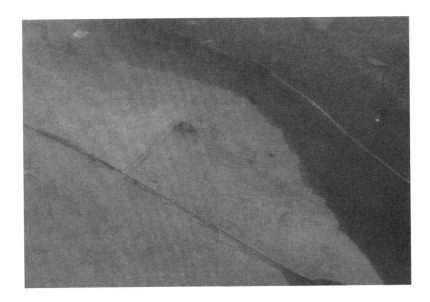

Sometimes you will find holes, cuts under puddles of water and they are not actively leaking. It may take a certain amount of water to push the water through because of positive static pressure. Remember, often we are dealing with layers of insulation and materials. Gravity can only do so much, and if your entry point is in a puddle, and it's not active, it's probably due to positive static pressure or being held back due to the amount of materials.

Remember that, Static pressure is how much air is being pushed in and pulled out of the building by the air-handling units. There are three kinds that affect the way certain roof leaks operate.

Positive static pressure is when there is too much air being forced into a building.

Negative static pressure when too much air is being exhausted out of the building.

Neutral static pressure. This is typical for open barn type buildings with open garage doors and windows.

It's easy to detect what type of static pressure a building may have. All you have to do is watch an Exit or Entry door as it opens and closes.

Positive static pressure: Door takes a long time to close, or refuse to shut all the way. Usually associated with tightly sealed buildings.

Negative Static Pressure: Door is pulled shut by a strong breeze and is difficult to open. Usually associated with tightly sealed buildings.

Neutral Static pressure: Door opens and closes with little or no effort. Usually associated with open buildings, like garages or a building that may have open windows or open access doors.

What does this mean to you? Sometimes it can mean everything. Let me give you a real life situation. Back in '89, one of my very best customers had a roof leak that was heavy and consistent. It showed up one night when the plant suddenly lost its third shift. Most of the machinery was lathes and presses and so on. The water from the roof leak covered the entire concrete floor.

The union employees refused to walk in what could be electrified water. Solving this problem was especially important to my helpless customer and myself. When you cannot fix a roof leak that shuts down 90% of a factory that employs 1200, you're in trouble. That customer is loosing thousands of dollars, a minute.

I would be at the property in the day during a heavy rain, and guess what? Not a drop! Could not understand what I was doing wrong. I searched this old rubber rooftop to bottom. Once we had half the company out on it. We did find a few things here and there, proclaiming, "This is it!" Again, it fooled us by never leaking during the day and only over night. Not just leak, but pour in.

One day, we got there before the regular businesses hours. Production started working about 7:00 a.m. Before production started the active roof leak was filling 2 barrels every 30 minutes. We know this because, one of the security people spent all night dumping these barrels with fork lifts and such.

Out of the corner of my eye, I saw a person turn on the main power supply to a large roof top unit. The leak stopped almost immediately. This made no sense. I then asked the gentleman to turn the power back off. Afterwards, the leak took off and began pouring in, again.

These units were about 80 feet away from the leak area. They until recently worked three full time shifts and the power was never turned off. In reality, this roof leak may have existed for 20 plus years. Only after they cut down to two shifts was the units then shut down, removing the positive static pressure that prevented water from entering the roof system.

We found a five-inch rip at the base of a wall flashing that you could stick a hand in. These vents were also located at the valley or lowest level of the roof. What did happen was while the units were running; the positive pressure was pushing back the water. This may seem a little weird, but you will find some instances where a large tear or rip will cause a very small leak, yet a small pinhole may pull in a ton of water, depends on static pressure.

These are the possible affects of static pressure as it relates to a roof leak. That is why understanding static pressure is critical to the over all quality of your investigation. Later we made the repair, and it never leaked again.

You may find buildings that are so air tight they maybe susceptible to mold, staining and items of that nature. In most cases your hole, cut or split will often be up slope from the problem area. If there are two roofs, for instance a built-up roof under a rubber roof, water can actually fill up and appear to travel up hill creating a Ramping up scenario.

You will often see troughing around drains, scuppers, and water heads, around HVAC units or where water travels down a central point. Dry troughing is common around roof hatches and walkways.

Dry troughing can lead you to places that are not causing the actual roof related problem. Wet Troughing is caused by an opening somewhere in the membrane, dry troughing never has an entry point, ever.

Here is where it gets difficult, you have to use your own judgment, and learn to feel with your feet. Dry insulation will definitely feel different from wet insulation. Most important too, is it will sound different as you walk across the surface of the roof.

When you walk on healthy insulation it will pop, crack and make a unique sounds, we will call this a perfect H tone. On the other hand, a healthy tone. Wet insulation makes little to no sound when walked on, and feels soggy or spongy. Dry insulation is crunchy and stiff, wet insulation is soft and mushy. There are also varying degrees of these two conditions.

Icy troughing can be very helpful, if you listen for it. When temperatures hit below freezing, you can feel and hear ice crunch under the roof surface. Sometimes you can follow the ice crunching sound to the entry point. Because of this, you can centralize on the problem easier and quicker. People complain about going out in extreme conditions, but these conditions can present things you will never see or hear on a warm clear summer day.

Troughing on graveled or ballasted roofs is very difficult to identify. You can, instead of moving tons of gravel and finding that troughed or damaged area walk the roof and feel the rock and insulation combination with your feet, this can save you a lot of time.

How much gravel do you want to move? Answer, as little as possible. Don't get me wrong, moving gravel is great exercise, builds stamina and muscle. Unfortunately, it is very harsh on our joints and bones. Just walking can wear out kneecaps and hipbones when carrying no extra weight at all. One large scoop of gravel can weigh up to 75 pounds! Of course mud, sand and other contaminates make the gravel much heavier.

Always look the roof over first. Troughing on a gravel roof can be identified by darker colors or dark shaded patterns on top of a graveled. You will usually notice light and dark shaded areas. The lighter the area, the less water sits, less carbon, which is a constant across the surface, or all roofs. The longer and deeper the gravel remains submerged, the darker the gravel. Let us look at a typical scenario.

Above we have a typical ballasted rubber roof. Notice the variations of colors, which indicate levels of moisture or water. I walked the roof and found this softer than average area. This troughed area runs from north to south and the decking of course runs opposite or perpendicular.

The best way to identify troughing on a ballasted roof is to walk known dry areas and getting familiar with the over all density. This makes it easier to identify troughed areas once you locate them.

Above I have moved a 2 foot by 6-foot area of gravel. Notice how the mud stain in the middle of the Troughed area is just inside of the wet area, or watermark. Watermark shows where and how high water has been collecting.

Rather than moving tons and tons of gravel, you must focus on the possibility of troughing. Only move swatches or centralized areas of gravel. Once you have identified a troughed area under gravel, move up hill. Follow the Troughing until it runs out or beyond into good solid roof. Usually trail of Troughed insulation will lead you to a larger area. When this happens, it means that the leak has been active for a long time. This may have even started when the building was constructed and one person dropped something on the last day of the job causing what eventually became a very established and damaging roof leak.

Above is where we followed the troughing up slope. We began the following this troughed insulation from the other end of the roof. Below is the entry point that we found that was the roof related problem. Notice, we did not move all the gravel.

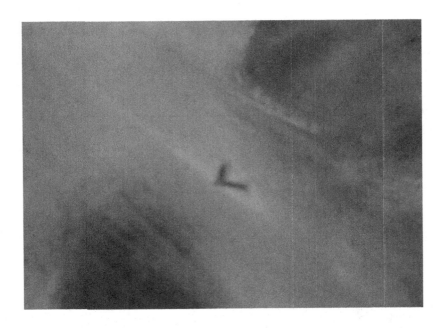

Rules for Ballasted Roofs

Never use a sharp or spaded type shovels. Always make sure that the shovel you are using has no edges that can cut the roof. Heavy course sand paper can often take care of this and use Aluminum shovels, less weight.

Never jab the shovel through gravel. Always use your foot, heel first and set a starting point by sinking your foot through the gravel and scraping the gravel away for a starting point to begin shoveling or moving gravel.

Never ignore penetrations close to Troughed areas, always clean the area around them.

When scraping across the roof surface always scrape towards you. Never scrape forward as you might accidentally open a lap or scrape into mechanical fastener causing an unseen entry point.

Can you not only see, and feel troughing on almost all types of roofs but also under the right conditions but you can actually hear it, so use it when you can.

Not all roof leaks will have troughing. This additional tool can help point you closer to the problem or entry point that you are specifically looking for.

Residuals from chapter 11

Troughing is a natural phenomenon that happens when insulation becomes damaged by moisture or weight causing a sunken or softened area of roof.

Two types of Troughing, Troughing, and Dry Troughing.

Conducting a Trough Search should be the first thing done after you have secured your search grid.

Troughing exists on all types of roofs that contain insulation or material similar to fiberglass or wood based products.

Troughing drops the R-Factor rating on all roofs dramatically.

Troughing can be identified on Ballasted Roofs by identifying dirty areas of sunken or discolored gravel.

Troughing causes fasteners to appear to back out and puncture membrane.

Not all roof leaks/roof related problems have troughing.

Chapter 12

Internal Thermal Identification

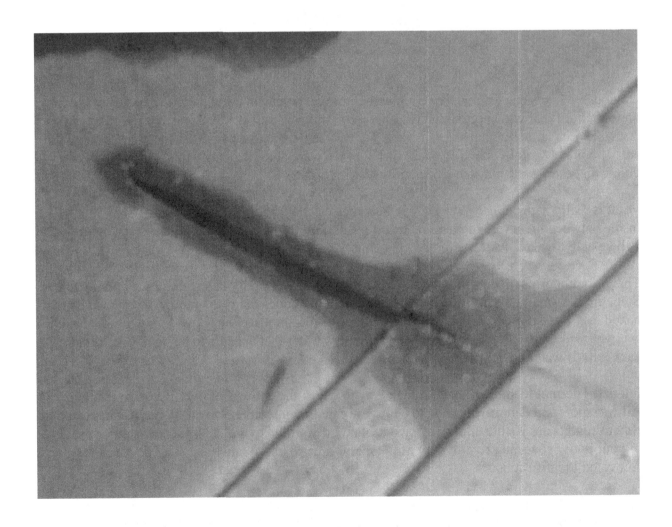

Another advanced search technique is Internal Thermal Identification, I.T.I., Internal (I), which means inside. Thermal (T), which of course is heat. Identification (I) is physically seeing and being able to understand what you are looking at.

Picture above shows I.T.I., on a non-reinforced rubber roof. Certain conditions create this often over looked opportunity. Usually early in the morning, after the dew begins to dry up, or after a rain event just ended, and the roof has begun drying up, are some of the conditions that create the opportunity for I.T.I. If the sun comes out and heats the surface of the roof, it will in turn heat up the water within the upper layers of roof, causing the water to expand and seep or bubble back out of an entry point.

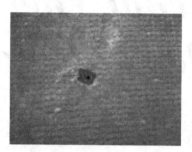

Obviously, this is entry point above in the membrane, it was found within 12 minutes of entering on to the roof that was approximately, 3000 thousand square feet. This was not found quickly because of its large size however, it was I.T.I. that sent us to this particular location. Found 18 entry points of various sizes. Because of I.T.I., we were able to identify many very small entry points that other wise may have been missed with out it.

What is really happening? When a leak becomes established, it will absorb and hold water inside between the layers of membrane and insulation. If the ambient conditions are right, you will be able to take advantage of this opportunity.

This is an important opportunity because the roof is inadvertently identifying Entry points for us. Sometimes a small hole, or a slice in the membrane that does not open enough to be seen by the naked eye, is easily seen with I.T.I. Even though you cannot see the actual hole with the naked eye, you will not be able to over look the reflective water that appears to be oozing, or draining back out. If water comes out, then water goes in.

Internal Thermal Identification is a quick way to check the entire roof over if you're in a hurry. All wet spots and damp areas need to be investigated. Sometimes you will look at an area and no water droplets are visible until you crawl around on your knees and with the pressure or weight of your body, you squeeze water out of the membrane. This situation is called, P.A.I., Pressure Activated Identification.

P.A.I. has helped me with porous rubber membrane that looked completely healthy otherwise. After I cut apiece out and held it up in front of the sun, I could see small Micro-Entry points, looked like stars in our galaxy. This of course is rare, but you will probably see it somewhere, and it is easy to over look because the Micro-Entry points are so very tiny.

Internal Thermal Identification can be accomplished by only a ten-degree temperature variation between the moisture inside the system and the outside ambient conditions. Springtime when the insulation is still cold, and the sun warms quickly, is your very best time to look for I.T.I. Anytime you have wet insulation, cool nights, warm bright mornings, you could have I.T.I., as an identifier.

After the early morning, the more you will loose the ability to utilize Internal Thermal Identification.

I.T.I. is also best used after a rain, while in the final drying stages of your roof. Areas that is still wet after most of the roof has dried up need to be circled and investigated. You can circle these identifiers with chalk or lay down a penny or quarter. We use very shiny markers as they are easier to see, once you walk away and have to come back.

If you have a bunch of entry points identified do not circle every single one. Usually easier and a lot less time to circle the cluster. I had a helper who was told to mark pinholes found on the roof membrane. I came back 20 minutes later, he had marked about 350. I told him I could get 350 with one circle! This would only take me 10 seconds. Do not waste time if you don't have to. He remarked they were just popping up. Sometimes you'll have that.

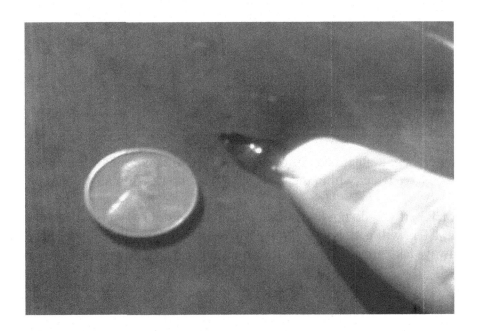

Here is an excellent example above. This is a small cut over a metal plate. Heat transfers through the screw/fastener up into the plate easily. The water that is over the plate expands and appeared to ooze out. I have video of water actually pulsating and almost appearing mechanical from an entry point.

The action that caused this pulsating appearance was indeed mechanical. Heating and cooling machinery or HVAC units and pressure in the building can create unusual types of reverse water activity. Reverse water activity is where the opening of the membrane is not covered, and the water expands outward through the top of the roof, rather than draining down into the building.

There is not enough pressure from the top of the roof system to push the water downward. Also, too little water for gravity to pull through.

Often when these types of roof related problems are repaired, they begin leaking, even though there is no water on the roof, only within the system. That is always a good sign, when the leak becomes active after a repair has been completed or applied.

I.T.I. is great under these ambient conditions, but what if you do not have the proper conditions and you know you have water within the system? What about artificially creating I.T.I.?

Do not attempt I.T.I., if you do not have water within the system. If it has been a while since any good rain event, I.T.I., will not happen. Using a propane torch is not recommended on most rubber roofs, always take great care when forced to utilize a heat source on any roof.

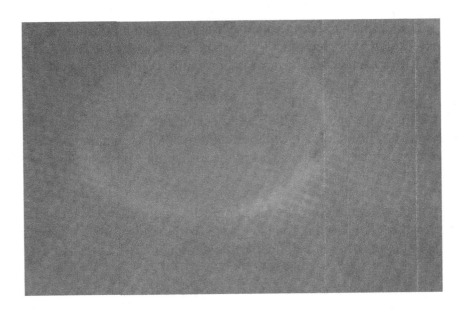

Time lapse of 2 seconds with a quick blast of a propane torch. I.T.I. will not work if the membrane is not directly making contact with the insulation.

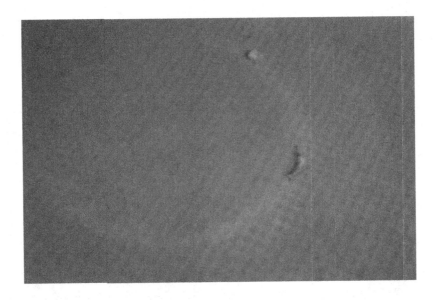

The insulation has to make contact with the membrane to create a positive static pressure point within the insulation and membrane. This pressure is what creates expansion and pushes the water back out.

If you use propane torches on the roof and do decide to push the envelope, there are some things you need to know. Never take any torch on any roof without fire extinguishers. Moreover, never use propane on Heat Weld systems, ever.

It will take only a few seconds to damage, melt or catch the membrane on fire. Most of us who live in the northern United States are often left with no other choice but to utilize a heat source like a propane torch every single day during winter months. Without it we are unable to make a living.

Membrane will pull tighter as it ages. This natural occurrence will be concentrated at the highest points of the insulation. The membrane will pull tight over the mountainous part of the insulation and never touching the valley areas of the insulation. Without this compression, I.T.I., will not be obvious or easy to find.

Again, this is just another scenario of why membrane does not make contact with the insulation well enough to provoke I.T.I. Even if you have water within the system, without that compression or pressure inside, you will not be able to utilize I.T.I., as an identifier.

Don't contaminate your search area

Remember; walk either on the dry portion or on the wet portion as not to get confused, with which is which.

Wet foot prints above. Below we have identified an entry point. Notice how they look so very similar.

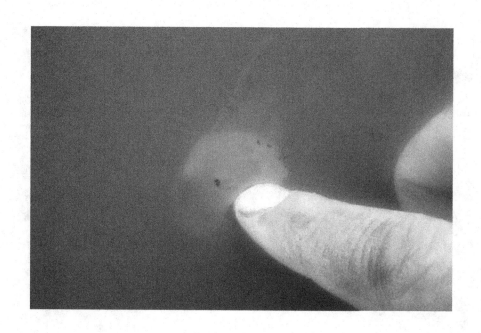

Residuals from chapter 12

Internal Thermal Identification is a natural phenomenon that happens when water within the top layers of roof just under the membrane become heated and expand due to a heat source either natural or artificial. This heating causes the moisture within the upper layers of the roof to expand and push back out of entry points.

Internal Thermal Identification will happen if, there has been a recent rain event, the outside conditions are cool, and you have a heat source on top of the roof surface such as early in the morning or the dry up time after a rain event when the roof is in its very last stages of drying up.

Internal Thermal Identification is most prevalent mostly in the spring and fall.

Morning Dew can mimic I.T.I., as the entry point will be the last thing to dry up on the roof surface.

Internal Thermal Identification does occur on graveled roofs and is often hidden.

If artificially creating the conditions of I.T.I., on the roof with a torch, do not attempt without a fire extinguisher as is not recommended.

Internal Thermal Identification is not prevalent on all roofs but is a reliable way to locate an entry point under the right conditions by identifying entry points that are too small to be seen with the naked eye.

Propane is not recommended for EPDM roofs, but can be utilized if done in a very safe manner.

Always have Fire Extinguishers available if you do attempt to utilize propane on the roof surface to artificially create I.T.I.

Propane torches are never to be utilized on any Heat Weld System.

Chapter 13
Sound Resonance

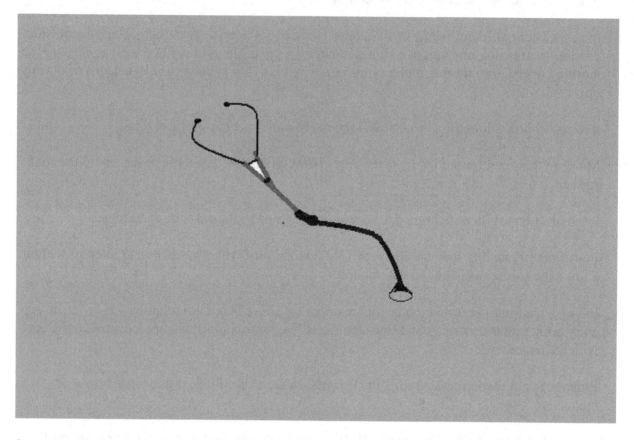

One more tool that may help in the end when it comes to searching out a roof related problem is Sound Resonance. Sound resonance is only possible with a Stethoscope. Usually meant for health care professionals, this simple tool can give you definitive answers.

One of the things learned over the years is that sound does not travel very well through wet insulation. Sounds crazy that someone would actually check that, but it's true, I did. Wet insulation will muffle the sound produced by machinery, and typical noises that go on inside a factory or business.

If you take a Stethoscope and put the sound intake end of it on the surface of the roof, it can indeed lead you to or away from wet insulation. Even if there was not many noises going on down below, there has usually been an over all roar within the building. That is if there is activity of any kind below.

This roar is the over all sound signature of the factory or business. Before you give up or go onto Surgical Intervention mode consider introducing a Stethoscope. It may be that little bit more information that you need, to solve the mystery.

A Stethoscope can also be utilized for identifying unusual or un-needed air intake around units. Of course, when air is pulled into a unit, air also pulls in water/rain.

Sometimes around access doors or attached skins, there can be voids where air is being pulled in because of the vacuum. You can't see it, and in most cases cannot hear it. With a Stethoscope, you can hear this unseen force that is not only pulling air from outside into the unit, but that same force is also pulling in moisture of all types.

Taking the microphone end of the Stethoscope around doors, tech screws along edges can tell you an awful lot. Quite a few roof related problems were solved by yours truly, only because my Stethoscope told me where the air was being pulled in at.

When should you use a Stethoscope? When you think it can give you an advantage. It's a small thing that can make a huge difference in helping us understand what is actually going on.

Stethoscopes are also handy during water testing at HVAC units. It can show you where the water needs to be applied to re-activate a particular roof leak. If you have discovered an area that you suspect of pulling in air, get permission, get the water hose and test your theory. If the roof related problem becomes active, take apart the unit as much as possible at the affected area and take many pictures of the actual activity.

You will not be utilizing Sound Resonance on every job or every day. Make sure you have a case for your Stethoscope and keep it close. Some people like to take them, just because, and there you are, out a Stethoscope. A good one costs about $100.00, but you can usually find them cheaper.

For many repair people and roofers, they are often dating health care professionals or know someone that they can get one from, free. Every couple of years or so, they will replace the one that they have and pretty much throw away the old one. Don't let them, ask and thou shall receive. Got mine for $10.00 from a nurse who just graduated nursing school and had to get a new one for her new high paying job. Her trash is now my treasure. And what a treasure it is to be capable of absolutely determining a cause that will lead to a conclusive solution.

My helper one time, while we were working at a doctor's office asked if they had an extra Stethoscope, he simply lied telling them his got broken. Nurse left for a minute and came back with one nicer than mine! He wore it like a doctor for a week.

Do not do that. Take it out when needed and keep it around your neck until finished. Do not lay it down or drop it, if at all possible. They do break. You are not required to have a Stethoscope, but if you want to take advantage of every opportunity, get one and take good care of it. They can last a very long time if treated with respect.

Sound Resonance has yet another use. Sometimes a location cannot be measured out. When that happens you can get an exact location of your entry point using sound resonance. In essence, we utilize Sound resonance in a way to identify our entry point locations when needed.

That is what were going to do. It is a simple thing but can be very helpful and some times necessary to do, under the some circumstances. You need one person on top of the roof relatively close to the exit point location, as it is downstairs. Then you need something to tap the bottom side of the decking with. Sound vibrations also travel through concrete decking as well. It will not be as loud, but effective enough to complete the task. That task is to identify the exit point exactly as it is on the roof.

Myself would have my helper to duct tape broomstick handles together end to end. Three or four broomstick handles would usually be long enough, or tall enough to reach the bottom side of the decking. It, whatever contraption you may be constructing has to be ridged enough to take the stress of tapping hard on the bottom side of the decking.

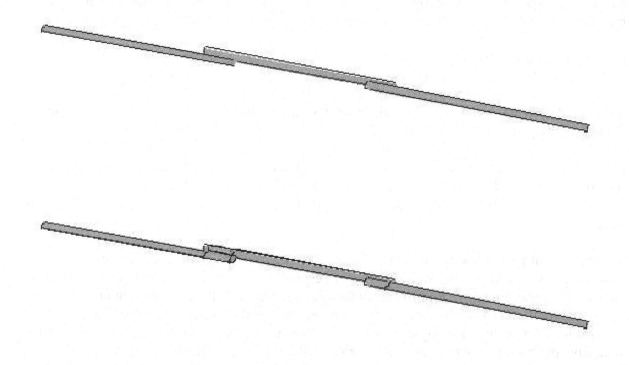

Above is how we would initially tape together handles to reach the bottom side of the decking. No one is going to be hauling a twenty-foot long pole on his or her work vehicle. If you are driving around in a flat bed, guess it would be possible. Here where we live, we drive average vehicles that are designed to carry certain sizes and certain weights safely. Paint handles can be purchased in different sizes and lengths. An 8 or 9 footer wouldn't be a bad thing to carry around as it extends to almost double its length.

The reason we utilize broomstick handles is that we usually have several of them lying around in our work vehicles. Some broomstick handles are threaded, those are the best to use. If you do have PVC type plastic tubing and are able to use that, please do. It does not matter what you make it out of, only that you can use it mark your dual point positioning when all other measurements fail to produce an entry point. The threaded wooden broomstick handles are not as heavy has the tapered broom stick handle. The threaded handle broomstick is usually thinner and easier to work with. Just tap the bottom side of the decking with your pole.

When you are done and you have confirmed an exact location, dismantle the long length rod. Un-tape it and return your broom stick handles to their original location in your work vehicle. This way, you are not searching for all the components the next time you need them. Do not forget we are trying to eliminate negative processes.

As before, this is to be used if you cannot get an exact location, or you feel uncomfortable with the location you have ended up with marked on the roof. It maybe necessary if you want a third opinion. A third opinion means just that. If you have already collected measurements, and your helper has collected measurements and you are still not producing any type of positive result, then use sound resonance.

Remember, when you collect measurements and you complete Dual point positioning, that's one opinion. When your helper collects his or her own set of measurements and has also completed dual point positioning, that is two opinions. Your third and final hope to locate the exact location, or exact flute of metal decking or a definitive location, is sound resonance. Utilizing it will be rare, but when needed, it is another option out there that you can take when the circumstances or situation is stacked against you.

When you're unable to collect slope information, which is difficult enough and can hamper but not kill your investigation. Not being able to confirm an exact location of an exit point can and will kill your investigation.

You're almost certain to make a return call when you're missing critical information. Dual point positioning is designed specifically to locate an exact thing. This thing, a roof related problem is the whole purpose of our attention. Let's do it right by collecting that information correctly and as completely as possible.

Never throw anything from the ground level at or to the bottom side of decking. It's dangerous and not very accurate. Property and persons can be harmed with one try. Don't do that.

Residuals from chapter 13

Sound resonance can be utilized two ways.

Stethoscope can differentiate between wet insulation and dry insulation.

Stethoscope can help identify vacuum leaks in or around all types of units, vents and heater house applications where there may be suspicion of that type of activity.

Stethoscopes can provide critical information when needed.

Always take good care of your Stethoscope and never loan it out.

You can get a Stethoscope from graduating nursing students, sometimes for free.

Do not wear your Stethoscope unless it is being used.

Stethoscope use is just another tool that may help tremendously when it comes to very difficult to locate non-roof related problems.

When constructing a long length rod to tap the bottom side of the decking, use the lightest and most rigid material you can find.

After locating the exact location of the exit point, dismantle the long length rod and return all the components to your work vehicle.

Never throw objects from the ground level to strike the bottom side of decking for any reason, it is dangerous and could damage property.

Chapter 14

Water Testing with Time Differentials

Water testing is a sure fire way to find a repeat or problematic roof related problem. That is if you know where to start and stop the process at the right time. It is very important that time differentials be utilized. What are time differentials and what is the proper way to conduct a water test? Began developing their use about 20 years ago for a customer who was installing some large smelters. If one drop of water got into the molten aluminum, there would be a large explosion that would kill many people.

They had not used the building or the space in a long time so they did not know if there were any roof leaks. I had done other repair work for this customer but had never been to this building before, and the weather had been dry for a few months. This makes it almost impossible to track any activity.

My first attempt went poorly. We soaked everything down and activated a roof leak but I could not tell where the Entry point was located. I broke it down to levels and allotted time for those levels. It is common sense, and there are rules you must follow, or your water test will fail.

The most important rule of all is making sure the customer is aware and gives permission to conduct a water test. The customer may have roof related problems over computers, machinery, etc. They may have to arrange to move the merchandise or cover it just in case you activate the roof leak. Do not blow anything up.

What you will be doing is creating a short and temporary, rain event. If you generate enough water you too, can activate and deactivate most roof related problems quickly and with a great amount of control.

Requirements

Must have permission to conduct a water test.

Must have water hoses and spray nozzle, and enough hose to reach.

You must have a competent person with you.

This person has to be at the water Exit area or bottom E location.

This person has to have a two-way radio or cell phone of some type. That person below at the bottom E has to inform the person at the top E the very moment the activity begins.

What we want is to activate, deactivate the leak and reactivate the leak to confirm its location.

There are 6 levels to a typical Water Test with Time Differentials. They go from negative 2(-2, to +4) to positive 4. It's just a way to accurately identify where any particular item may have a problem without error or guess work.

Typical Water Test for Drains/Roof Conductors. First, we confirm the pipe isn't cracked, about 5 to 10 minutes is required. Drainpipe equals, level -2.

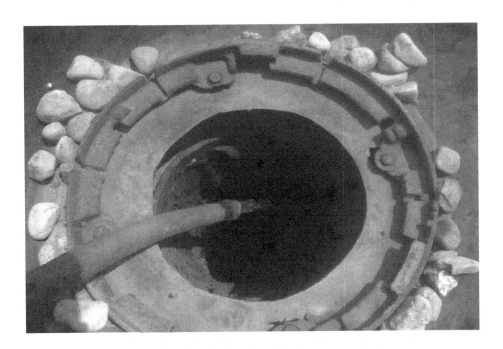

Above we are testing the seal between the roof membranes, water block and drain pipe that is identified as level -1. About 10 minutes is required below, flooding out the area at the drain ring, level 1. About 15 minutes is required. We have cleared this item properly.

A typical water test has 6 separate levels and appropriate times for these levels. You do not want to start from the top and work your way down. This defeats the purpose of the exercise.

Level 1

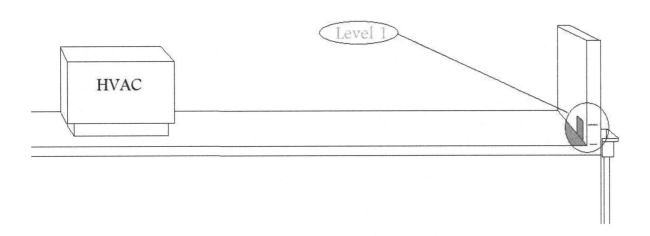

Anytime you are conducting a water test you will begin at the lowest point that in this case is the scupper or drain area. After completing level -2,-1, and level 1 around the main drainage area, move to level 2, the roof surface.

Level 2

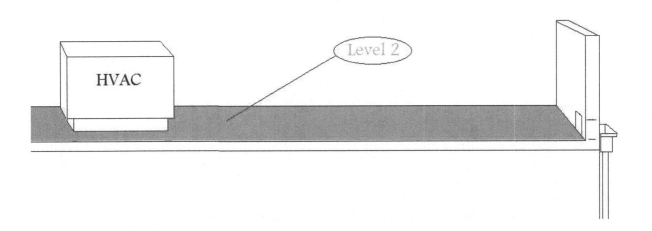

Level 2 covers the surface of the roof only. 10'by 10'areas per 15 minute time differentials. Anything above the roof surface is to be ignored.

Level 3

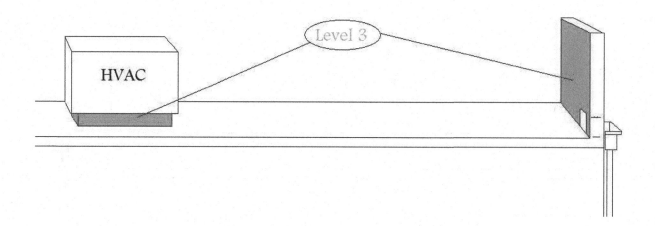

Level 3 is specifically for wall flashings only. Do not spray or pour water beyond these wall flashings. Time differential 15 minutes.

Level 4

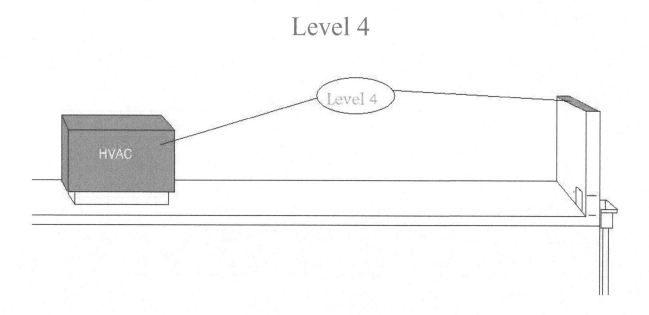

Level four covers HVAC units, penetration and coping metals. All items above the wall flashing, roof surface and drains should be eliminated systematically. In addition, because roof leaks take a certain amount of time to become active patience is required to fulfill the needed variances. It may take 30 minutes to activate a leak.

These are the basics, but what about sloped roofs? This is where the systematic part comes in handy. You will soak the area in what size patterns you prefer. About 15 minutes of constant flooding per level should activate most roof related problems.

Above where all water tests start, level one at drains/scuppers.

Below we moved only about 10 foot inward and upward onto the roof surface.

Above we moved our water test location further uphill. Below looking from the other direction, we have worked our way up to an HVAC unit.

Moving upward still around HVAC units. Notice the walk pads? Anytime you have a common walkway, this area must be investigated vigorously.

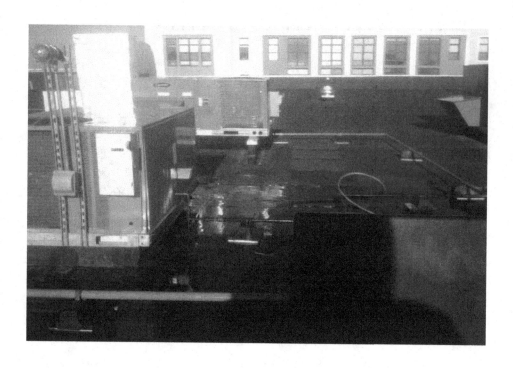

Above we are still heading up hill at 15-minute intervals moving about 8 to 10 feet. At this point, we activated the roof leak. That's when the water stops and the search begins.

Always nice when a plan comes together. After shutting down the water, we combed the roof and found multiple entry points. Because the roof is reinforced membrane, the entry points were very difficult to see.

Actual tear in roof

If you find yourself with a low water supply, use your water hose to make a dam. You can add an inch of heavy water to the surface and control the amount of water.

Ballasted roof water testing requirements

Discover the slope or fall of the roof

Do not remove gravel

Start at your lowest point

Allow extra long water intervals

The reason for the extra long time intervals is that is so much fine dust, dirt and other biological elements will absorb a lot of water. Mater of fact that fine dust and dirt will slow down the saturation rate of the water as it attempts to soak your roof surface.

Teaching others how to perform this properly, one thing that I have noticed is that most people just wet the gravel down. Getting the gravel wet will do nothing substantial as far as water intake is concerned. Ever been on a roof during a good soaking rain event? If you have not then you have missed a lot. It takes time for water to saturate dust/dirt and bio debris on the roof surface, then water has to get into the system.

Always saturate ballast/gravel completely. Above, substandard saturation. Below we have a ballasted roof saturated enough for a proper Water test.

Following the rules of water testing, we activated the roof leak. We removed the gravel at the area of activation, below our entry point.

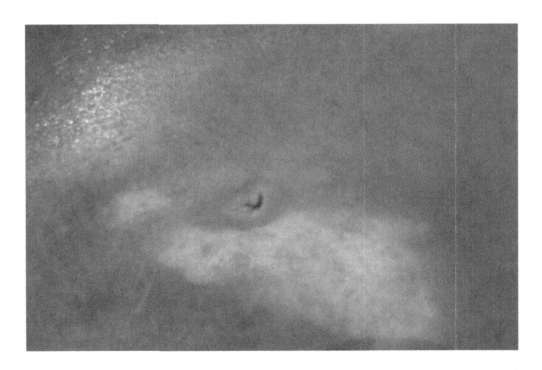

Residuals from chapter 14

Water Testing with Time Differentials is defined as utilizing a controlled man made rain event in a systematic way in hopes of activating a roof related problem based on average start times of known roof leak activation ratios.

Water Testing with Time Differentials is utilized to separate the distinct causes of a roof related problem, usually for determining a roof leak from a unit leak.

Water Testing with Time Differentials is also utilized for activating a non-active roof leak so an investigation can be started.

Water Testing with Time Differentials is to be completed with a minimum of two men and two way radios or cell phones. As soon as activation begins, the water is shut down. This saves many wasteful trips up and down the ladder.

Water Testing with Time Differentials is to be utilized when all over opportunities have been exhausted in relation to searching out a roof related problem.

Chapter 15

Surgical Intervention

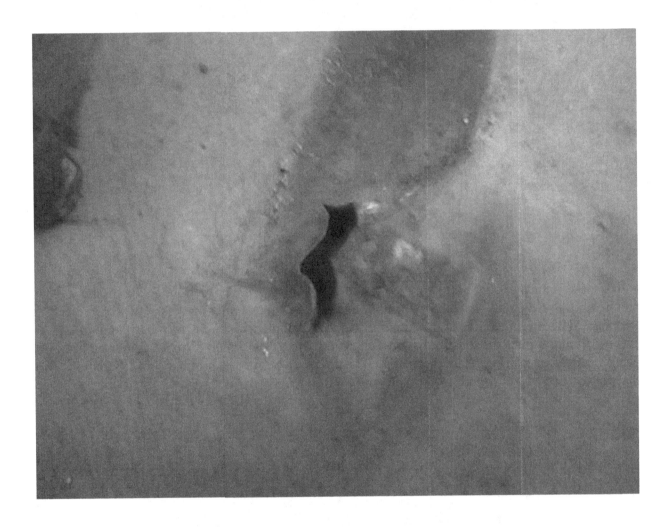

    Surgical Intervention is a sure shot way to track activity, but with a price. Always triple check your measurements before you begin S.I. Yes, I said that correctly. Check and confirm your location measurements again before you take on this task. This specific task creates additional Entry points in the main roof membrane that are permanent. The epidermis layer of any older rubber membrane roof naturally contracts as the oils dry out and can become unpredictable. To prevent any unforeseeable factors, here are some common sense actions to take into consideration, when surgically opening the roof membrane.

When cutting into the membrane of a roof always make sure you round your cuts.

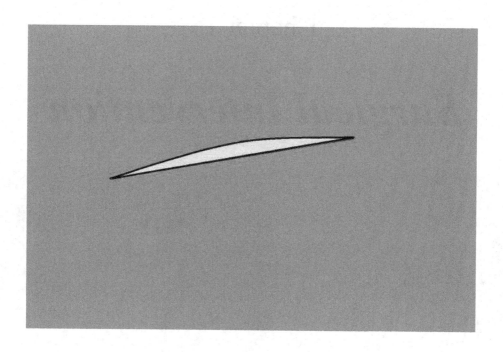

Blue represents membrane and Yellow represents insulation

Never make jagged or sharp broken glass looking cuts in any rubber membrane like in the picture above. Some like me have witnessed a large rip in the membrane years after a core cut was made. Because the ends of the cut/slice were not rounded, when the roof began contracting and expanding it pulls the membrane causing the cut, rip to tear much further than the actual patch that was over the core cut originally. This looks ugly when you find a rip in membrane that was caused by not rounding your cut.

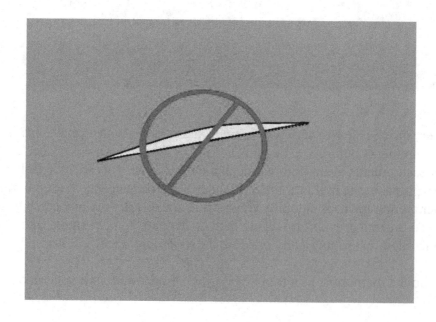

Never leave cuts or slices as in the illustration above. Below is the correct way to prevent ripping, tearing of membrane.

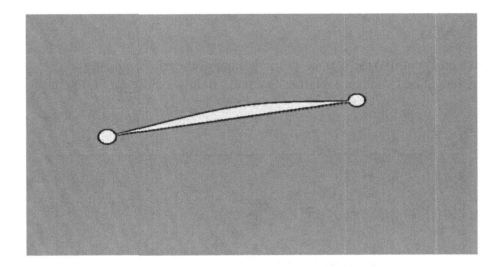

Some people make a small opening like the examples in illustration 1,2g. Sometimes, we have to open up the roof, and see with own eyes exactly what is going on, inside the roof.

If you have to open the roof up make, sure you have more than enough material to cover the new man made Entry point. Some may open up several places to confirm or witness the Path of travel or to confirm dry/wet Troughing. Only open what you need to open. Do not walk around the roof creating openings all over the place, as this can quickly get out of hand.

You may have already suspected that water is traveling along metal decking and need to confirm which direction it may be coming from to point you in the right direction as to begin your search.

You may have to cut out some of the insulation and look directly at the deck. Hopefully you will have water inside somewhere. Surgical intervention is not useful if there is no water within the roof system. Stains discovered may have been from previous roof leaks that could have had their source halted.

What should an opening look like and how should it be repaired? By now, you probably know that this field guide is not about how to make a patch. That information is up to the actual manufacturer of the material. When you do make an Entry point follow these rules. All Surgical Intervention openings are made in an H pattern.

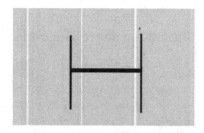

Above we have an H-cut into the surface or membrane of the roof in illustration. Notice that the length and width are relative or equal. Below a close up of our surgical entry point.

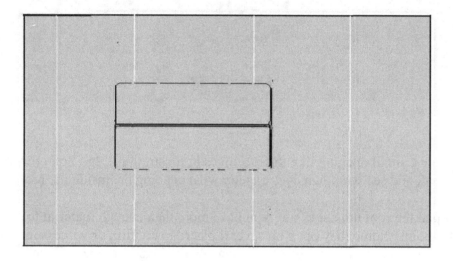

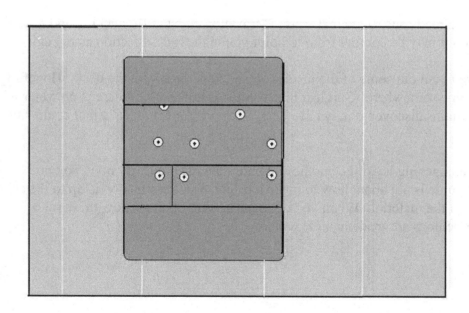

Above we have surgically opened the roof surface. Whether you are looking for wet insulation or maybe a path of travel that is below the insulation make sure you cover this opening completely and properly. Do not simply strip this area together with cover type tape and leave it.

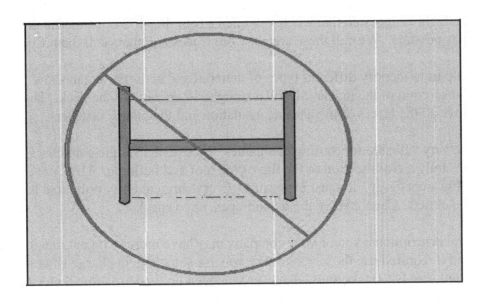

Above in illustration 7g, is how not to cover a surgical Entry point. Below in illustration 8g, we have the proper type patch complete with safeties at each corner.

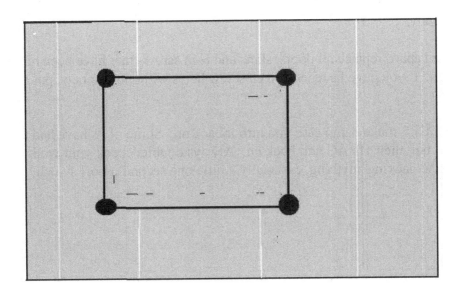

Without the proper means of attachment, this patch may flutter around. This lack of attachment also affects the integrity of the roof. Always add additional fasteners and plates where need as in our illustration.

Never jab the scissors into the membrane and start a journey to the other end of the roof. If you have gone to the point of utilizing Surgical intervention, make sure this action is done efficiently, not quickly. It's highly suggested that when you open a roof that you open the smallest, yet accessible area as possible. We call these areas, "Core Checks. Others call them Core Cuts.

Core Checks help us to identify different types of material and activity. It can show Piggybacking, absorption of the insulation and a straight down view of the deck. That is if you are able to remove all the layers of membrane, insulation and the plates, fasteners.

Core Checks are very valuable for roofing companies because, that single core check has information. It's truly a cross section of the life of the roof and building. The Core check is essentially roofing archeology. It's just expensive. Every surgical entry point that has been opened has to be closed. Cannot leave the wound open, so to speak.

These are general descriptions; you or your company may have more stringent repair application requirements and if required use those, make sure you ask some one in charge what the protocol may be. The point here is to make sure what ever you open up, you are more than capable of covering back up in a complete and professional manner. No one wants a half ass job, and no repair person wants to worry about if the opening that they have made may fail and come back to haunt them.

Opening up HVAC units is also a form of surgical intervention. I really cannot give you good descriptions or illustrations to prevent problems if you happen to have to open up a unit and look inside. Good advice is to have an HVAC technician on site, but in the real world, you won't have that opportunity.

If you take the unit apart, replace all doors, skins and tech screws that have been removed during your investigation. If you have fastener or tech screw holes without fasteners, put a new screw into the opening.

If you turn the unit off, make damn sure you turn it back on. Some of us have had to drive back 150 miles only to turn their HVAC unit back on. Always double, check your work and make sure that you are not lacking anything, especially a little one second on/off switch.

Residuals from chapter 15

Surgical Intervention is to be utilized when all else has failed.

Do not attempted Surgical Intervention if you do not have the proper materials needed to repair or close the opening.

Always round all cuts and slices at their end points to prevent tearing or ripping.

Make all openings into an H-shape to allow full view within the roof.

Never strip in these types of openings. Cover completely with the same type of roof membrane, no flashing or cover type tape should ever be utilized to dry this type of application in.

Utilize safeties, and reattach all anchor points.

Always close all units, penetrations you open up, and turn on units you shut off.

Chapter 16
Ratios Rule

    Ah, love ratios, and you will too. This is why. Regardless of what type of roof, there will always be an E over E ratio when we have a legitimate roof leak. In addition, regardless of what type of roof you may have there will always be an Over all Ratio. Finally, to complicate things further we have the Start time Ratio. The E over E ratio discloses the actual difficulty value or rate of the repair. The Over All Ratio tells us in advance the difficulty level of any particular type of roof. The Start Time Ratio tells us what action maybe going on within the roof system.

One gives us warning as what to expect, the other tells customers how hard we had to work to solve the roof related problem. They are not necessary for solving every roof related problem but will give us more awareness and insight in to the situation especially, if we know what to expect depending on the type of rain event we are experiencing due to Time start Ratio, and the Over all Ratio as placed by the E over E ratio.

Getting a hint as whether you should begin your search in a valley or low-lying area or up high on a tapered system, or maybe a hint about how lengthy the path of travel could be, may make all the difference when it comes to securing a definite, and accurate entry point location.

E over E Ratio

Let's start with one of the last things you will do, obtain your E.O.E ratio. The E over E ratio is the distance between the entry point and the exit point as measured on the roof surface. Very rare will you see and entry point directly above the exit point. This would be a 1:1 E over E ratio, or a perfect 1:1 E.O.E. Ratio. Also known as a Bulls-eye.

Whether it is metric or standard, it is completely acceptable and that call is up to you.

This is one of the many good reasons why we need a compass. Not only does this type of measurement tell us the ratio between the entry point/hole or slice in relation to the leak/exit point but this exit point to entry point ratio can also tell us the direction of the two in relation to the roof.

Always using your true north we always base this either parallel or perpendicular and finally diagonally. There are always crooked tracks or paths that water takes while traveling within the system, especially on the decking.

The E over E Ratio has no effect on the "Path of Travel, which we will go over later. This simple ratio will always be your final measurement after the entry point has been secured. The smaller the number, the less time involved in solving the problem. The more diagonal, the more difficult and more time consuming to solve. Fact is, all perpendicular or parallel roof related problems are much easier to find or solve, than diagonal. Diagonal roof related problems are the most expensive, due to additional time spent during the physical search part of the task.

If that same entry point were running parallel to the exit point, this would be a parallel expression. This would be expressed as a parallel ten to one E over E ratio. It would also be written out as a 10—1 E over E ratio.

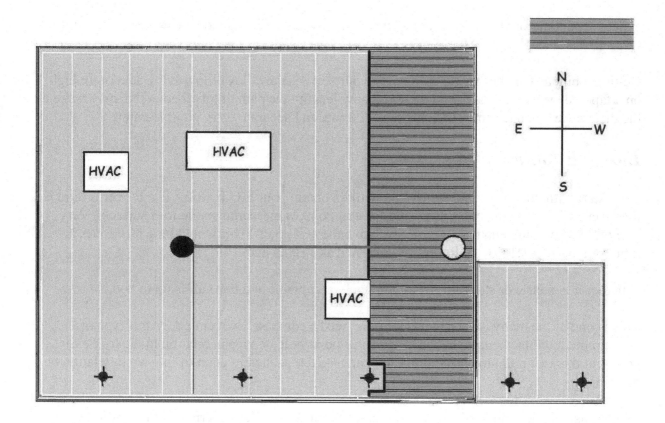

In this cut away roof/deck example above, our measurement between the entry point in yellow, and the exit point in black, is 27' feet or 9 meters. Notice that both entry and exits point are, or about within the same flute or run of metal decking (grey). This would be a parallel, twenty seven to one E over E ratio or nine to one E over E ratio.

This would be written out as E.O.E = 27—1. Or if in metric, it will be written out as E.O.E. = 3 —1. Do not sweat an off set of a foot if the entry point and exit point are not within the same flute of metal decking Always disregard inches and centimeters. As long as it is in an overall parallel state, that is close enough in the roof world.

This particular ratio tells us there is no piggybacking, or unusual slopes. It also tells us that there is probably one layer of insulation. This also tells us that the repair was relatively simple. This does not mean it was easy. After all, there is travel time to the location, meeting with the customer, inspection of the activity. Taking measurements, checking for slopes then taking these measurements on the rooftop, just to get started on the repair.

Afterwards you will create a search area/grid area, utilize perpendicular and parallel strategies, and conduct a trough search. Utilizing the proper search techniques and securing defective or deficient items, and finally making permanent repairs. Of course, you still have to down load un-used materials and tools, safety equipment. All within about a three-hour period. That is still plenty of work to fill in that three hour typical repair time.

168

Is three hours enough time? As long as you focus and go through each step competently, beating this deadline is easy. Many times under these circumstances, we would usually secure measurements and the entry point or points within an hour of arriving.

There will be some people who might say that they have been on a single layered roof with one layer of insulation, typical flat decking and yet had to spend a lot of a time finding the entry point. They probably were not focused enough, did not have the proper information, or maybe over looked the problem originally. There are so many things that can go wrong, that is why we need to focus in on the task at hand. How about a diagonal E over E ratio?

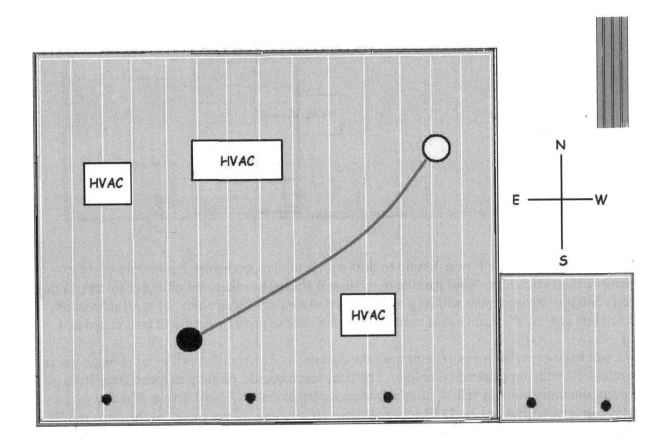

Above we have an example of a diagonal E over E ratio. In our illustration above, the entry point in yellow and the exit point in black with a blue line showing our path of travel. Piggybacking can distort this ratio dramatically and appear to make no sense how the water gets from one location to the other.

Our distance between the entry point and exit point is 27 feet. It would be expressed as, a diagonal 27\1 E over E ratio. It would be written out as, 27\1 E over E ratio. This also tells customers and employer that it was a difficult problem to solve. In reality, this diagonal ratio is about five times more difficult to solve than a parallel E over E ratio. If metric, it would read out as 9\1 E.O.E. Ratio.

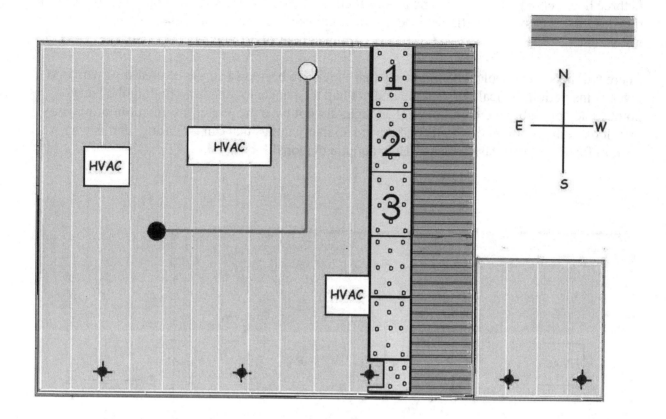

By far the most difficult E over E ratio to deal with is the Perpendicular E over E ratio. We measure this differently. Your parallel number will always be measured in feet or meters. You perpendicular measurement will rely on insulation placement and spacing. A typical sheet of insulation is 4' by 8'. Each board running perpendicular to problem area will be counted as 1.

We still have a parallel measurement from the decking of 27' from the exit point in black where it intersects with our perpendicular line. There are three boards, running perpendicular from or toward our entry point in yellow. Expressed as, a perpendicular 27 to 3 E over E ratio. Alternatively, written out as, 27⌋ 3 E over E ratio. If it were a mirror image of the same roof leak from a different direction, it would be 27 ⌊ 3 E.O.E. This Perpendicular type of ratio is the most difficult to solve. About ten times more difficult than a parallel ratio.

If someone looks up the work you did on a particular roof, and look at the ratio information, they are better prepared to discus and evaluate the time spent for the actual repair, and the difficulties involved. This also prepares us for the next time we go back for a new roof related problem on the same roof. In essence, the E over E ratio is a difficulty rating tool, and this tool justifies our time spent for our customers.

Most roofing companies consider this information important, the customer wants to know how difficult the repair may or may not have been. They also want to know if you are actually working while you are on their roof. These ratios clarify and justify your time no matter what that time is.

A typical repair person can solve a simple roof related item with a parallel E over E ratio rating in relatively short time, but solving the perpendicular and diagonally generated roof related E over E ratios, that is major bragging rights. Just because others do not recognize it, this does not mean you have to ignore your hard work and efforts. This type of information will prove that to your customer that you are damn serious about your craft, always keep this information available. After a while, you will begin relying on it. Its just part of the over all connection that ties everything together.

Descriptions for E over E Ratios

Parallel Ratios are the least difficult to search out and solve. Rated lowest on the difficulty scale. Justified time equals 3 hours or less per two men.

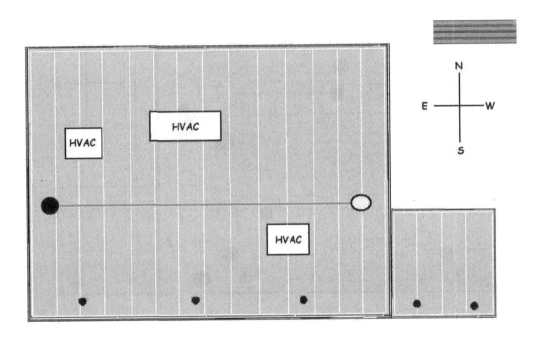

171

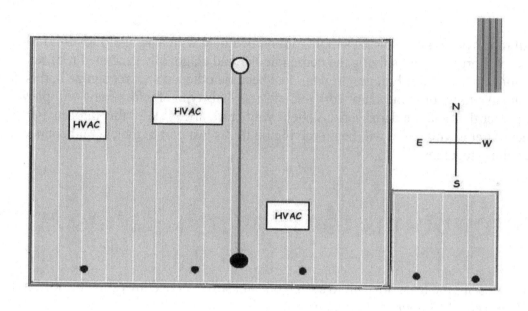

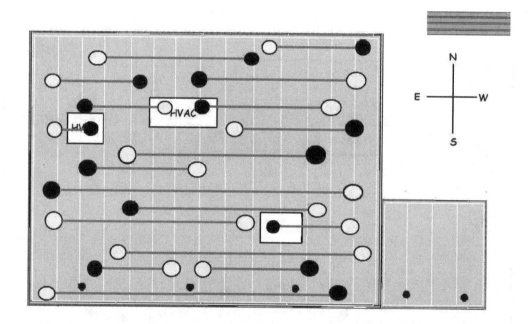

Above, we have a complete options map. This is to show you the endless possibilities. If you go to any type of roof that has a 1:1 over all Ratio chances are very good that your E over E ratio will run parallel to the decking.

Exit points are marked in yellow and Entry points are marked in black. Notice how some of the paths of travel from an Entry point to an Exit point will sometimes end up directly under a unit. This sometimes can causes false positives. Makes someone think that a unit maybe leaking when in fact it is a legitimate roof leak.

Perpendicular Ratios are the second most difficult to search out and solve. Rated number 2. Justified time equals 2 to 4 hours search time per two men. Remember that perpendicular paths of water travel can move from one end of the building to the other.

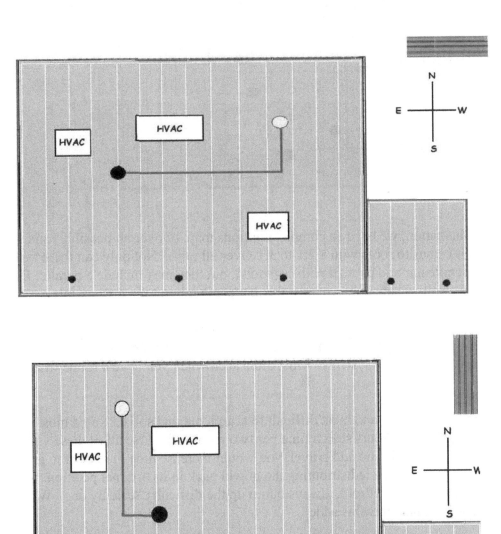

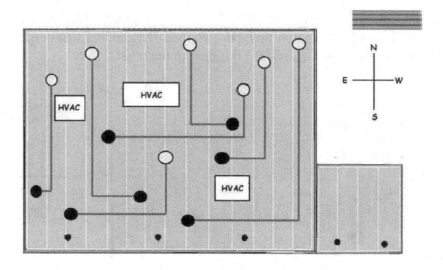

Above in our illustration, we have an complete options map, or over all possible routes that can be taken when it comes to roofs with a 2:1 to 3:1 Over all ratio. Not only can these types of roofs have perpendicular and parallel paths of travel, but they may include a parallel E over E or parallel routes as well. Chances are against that happening, but it maybe possible.

Looks like a computer circuit board doesn't it? As before there are over a million other possible outcomes, these are just to get your brain juices flowing. This type of ratio is often seen on tapered systems and dual roof systems. Most often seen when you have a rubber roof over a built-up roof.

Diagonal Ratios are the third and most difficult to search out and solve. Rated most difficult. Justified time equals 4 to 6 hours search time per two men. Of course all of these variables so far show roofs minus gravel. If you add gravel, you would increase time in respect to gravel removal and search time, then redistributing the gravel back in its original position. Any time you have gravel on any type of roof, always bump up the difficulty scale by one. What was a 1:1 would become a 2:1 when gravel is added.

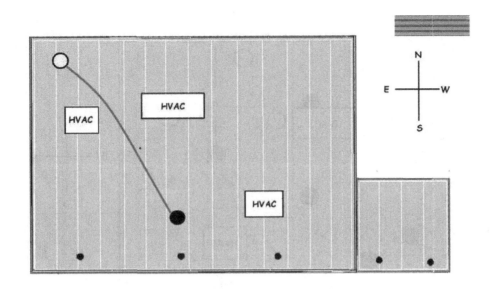

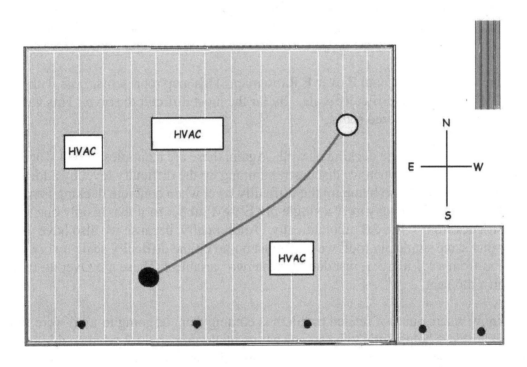

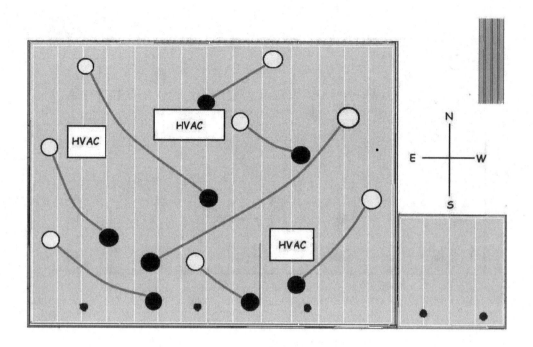

Above we have another Diagonal E over E Ratio map. This map represents roofs with an over all ratio of 3:1 to 4:1 on the difficulty scale. By far the most difficult to solve. This will happen on slightly sloped, multi-layered roofs.

4:1 is often seen with concrete decking as well. Again, these are examples of real world situations. Just like before when we discussed bumping up the difficulty level by adding gravel/ballast, you to will also bump up the difficulty level when concrete decking is part of the equation. Even though you may have a single ply EPDM rubber roof that is only one roof, if it has gravel, it goes from 1:1 to 2:1 automatically. Additionally, because we also have a concrete deck under that same single ply roof, we also must bump up the difficulty scale by one more. It will then read from a 1:1 to a 3:1, just due to those two variables. These are Over all ratios, we'll get to that in a moment.

We never know where our roof related problem is coming from or going to until were finished with the task. It does help a little to be somewhat mentally prepared for what could be a bad situation. Preparation is an important part of any investigation, the more prepared you are the better the outcome.

Another ratio we will be dealing with is the, "Over all Ratio." This over all ratio will change with, the type of insulation, how many layers of insulation and what type of decking is present. This is to be a difficulty-rating tool, but in advance. This rating tool is for roofs not worked on yet or to be worked on. This ratio is based on the variables of the type of roof put forth on a scale from easiest to most difficult.

The easiest will be 1:1 up to most difficult 4:1. 1:1 over all ratios will be your quickest, simplest and least time spent for a typical roof repair. Of course, a 4:1 over all ratio tells us that we have more variables to deal with, and a larger amount of time and effort.

The more roofs you have, the higher the over all ratio. The more layers of insulation, the higher the over all ratio. The tighter the laps or edges of decking, again, the larger the over all ratio and the larger the search field. Understanding all of these ratios together can be over whelming at first, but this is what we should expect as we move from roof to roof.

These over all ratios are relative to materials and circumstances taken into consideration from real world applications and investigations. Anytime you go to a roof leak call, or investigate a roof related problem, you will use this O.A.R. to plan accordingly and to ensure a complete investigation without needlessly wasting time.

Over All Ratios

1:1 O.A.R., fall within these parameters

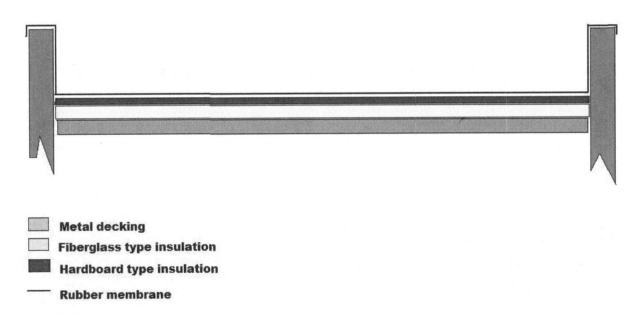

- Metal decking
- Fiberglass type insulation
- Hardboard type insulation
- Rubber membrane

*One layer of membrane or one roof.

*Non-ballasted or mechanically attached, fully adhered.

*One layer of insulation (usually fiberglass type insulation).

*Metal decking with a high to medium-sloped.

*Maximum of 6 or less penetrations.

*Heat Weld, Built-up Single-Ply, Torch down roofs also covered under 1:1 O.A.R.

*Fully adhered roofs, with one layer of membrane and insulation, with a typical metal deck is also covered under this O.A.R. of 1:1.

*Spaghetti and resin deck combination with one layer of insulation and one layer of membrane is also categorized as a 1:1 O.A.R.

*Time typically spent, three hours per two men.

*Difficulty level: Easy.

2:1 O.A.R., fall within these parameters

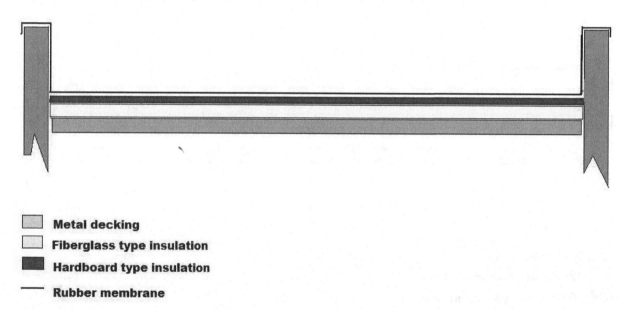

- Metal decking
- Fiberglass type insulation
- Hardboard type insulation
— Rubber membrane

*One layer of membrane or one roof, with light gravel.

*Non-ballasted upper layer with original roof under newer roof.

*Two layers of insulation, (usually one to two layers of fiberglass under one layer of fibered).

*Metal or wood decking with medium low to slight slope.

*Minimum of 12 and up to18 penetrations.

*Time typically spent, about three to four hours, per two men.

*Difficulty level: easy to medium difficulty.

*Fully adhered, one to two layers of insulation on typical metal or wood deck is also recognized under this ratio of 2:1.

*Spaghetti decked roofs lack a media to produce a path of travel within the system, but is covered under this ratio if you have a tapered system or more than one roof on top of the spaghetti deck.

3:1 O.A.R., fall within these parameters

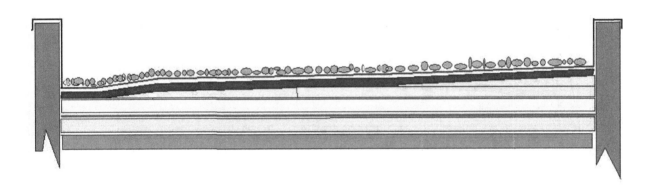

▢ **Metal decking**

▢ **Fiberglass type insulation**

■ **Hardboard type insulation**

— **Rubber membrane**

— **Old built-up roof**

▢ **Fiberglass or Recycled wood Insulation**

⬚⬚⬚ **Gravel or rocks**

*More than one layer of roof, ballasted with metal decking.

*Medium to heavily ballast, with one layer of insulation and wood decking.

*Tapered system or multiple layers of insulation.

*At least 18 and up to 30 penetrations.

*Built-up roof with EPDM roof over top is also covered under this protocol.

*Torch down and emulsion type applications under EPDM roofs are associated with this ratio.

*Time typically spent, three to six hours, per two men.

*Difficulty level: Very Difficult.

4:1 O.A.R., fall within these parameters

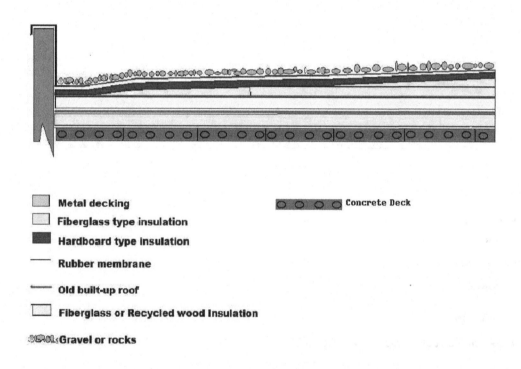

Metal decking

Fiberglass type insulation

Hardboard type insulation

Rubber membrane

Old built-up roof

Fiberglass or Recycled wood Insulation

Gravel or rocks

Concrete Deck

*Two roofs or more with ballast and metal decking.

*Heavily ballasted, one layer of roof and concrete decking.

*Tapered systems put down over solid concrete decking.

*Metal, wood or concrete decking with a very low to flat slope.

*Excessive amount of penetrations of more than 30.

*Time typically spent, five hours, up to what could be days.

*Difficulty level: Extremely Difficult.

Obviously, a ballasted two-layered roof on top of a concrete deck will be a more difficult investigation in contrast then a mechanically adhered one layered roof on a metal or wood-decked roof.

These combinations are for you to know what the difficulty level is in relation to the type of roof you are about to be working on.

There is still another ratio to be concerned about. This ratio is probably the most important ratio of all. The Start Time Ratio tells us very quickly, what we may be dealing with. Unfortunately, you can only get this ratio if someone is paying attention.

Thankfully, many people do pay attention. You have to ask those who do, this question. How long after the rain started did the leak become active?

You cannot depend on one eyewitness; ask everyone who may have been witness to the activity the same exact question. This time frame can decide whether the roof leak is, legitimate or non-roof related. In some cases, it can give us a hint as to the location of the entry point.

These are Time Differentials based on commonalities. These commonalities specifically relate to the weather and the materials of the roof in a whole were constructed from, sloping and reservoir factor in accordingly. Pay attention to weather reports. All roofers and repair people do pay attention to the weather report as a requirement, if he or she wants to know how to dress for working outside at least.

Regardless of what type of material the roof was constructed from, or the amount of rain depending on the type of event, there will always be a certain amount of time from the start time of the rain event, until the time it takes for water to travel out of the decking or that time that the leak became active. There will always be a start time.

Start time for a roof leak begins when rain begins hitting the roof surface. It is not when water begins dripping inside the building. That is the end result of the roof leak in question. Ironic how the last thing on a list that confirms the roof related activity, is the first thing on our list when we begin to search them out.

If the amount of time changes for the same type of roof with the specific combination of commonalities, it's for a good reason.

Differences such as the path of travel, reservoir expansion or multiple layers of insulation or material can delay this start time tremendously.

An average rain event will activate a roof leak that, has a Parallel E.O.E., Ratio of about 15 feet, and has non-absorbent insulation with a high to medium slope deck, in about 5 minutes. If longer, there may be reservoirs, and longer paths of travel.

This average start time ratio is dependent on two aspects. First, the amount of rain at any given weather event, or how much. Another aspect is the amount of time at any given weather event, or how long. Most importantly is how the water reacts once in the system.

A path of travel takes a lot of water just to prime the deck surface before water can begin to flow and pass beyond that level. Try an experiment; take a cup of water outside. Find some blacktop or concrete, walk slowly while pouring out the water in a straight line on the hard surface while keeping a constant stream.

You can see how much water it takes just to travel a few feet. When you see a barrel being filled by a strong and constant stream of water, think how much water it takes just to get the action started, let along how much more it will have to take to keep it active until, it exhausts all of its resources.

Average Rain/Ratio Rates by Description

Mist
About an eight of an inch of rain per hour.

Light rain Event
About a quarter of an inch of rain per hour.

Average rain Event
About a half inch of rain per hour.

Moderate rain Event
About three quarters of an inch of rain per hour.

Heavy rain Event

About an inch of rain per hour.

Monsoon Rain Event
About three to five inches of rain per hour.

Start Time Ratios

Average Activity Start time on roof type 1:1

Monsoon Rain Event
About three to five inches of rain per hour
Actual Leak Start Time
Less than one minute

Heavy Rain Event
About an inch of rain per hour
Actual Leak Start Time
About two to three minutes

Moderate Rain Event
About three quarters of an inch of rain per hour
Actual Leak Start Time
About four minutes

Average Rain Event
About a half inch of rain per hour
Actual Leak Start Time
About five minutes

Light Rain Event
About an quarter of an inch of rain per hour.
Actual Leak Start Time
About ten to fifteen minutes

Mist
About an eight of an inch of rain per hour.
Actual Leak Start Time
About thirty to forty-five minutes

*Average Rain Event

Immediate Activity Time Start for roof type 1:1

If leak activity was almost immediately after the rain event began, usually means it may not be roof related. This could indicate the entry point and exit point are very close to each other, no Path of travel or Reservoir. Could be a Perfect 1:1, E.O.E. Ratio. Possibly an HVAC, unit leak, or O.S. Could also be an entry point in the bottom of a valley or low-lying area.

Average Activity Time Start for roof type 1:1

If the leak activity takes about 5 minutes, we know that we most likely have an average Reservoir and/or a Path of Travel. Could have small amount of Piggybacking, or small Secondary reservoirs.

Longer activity time start for roof type 1:1

If the leak takes longer than 20 minutes to become active, it could mean that you have a very long path of travel. Maybe an extra large Reservoir. Possibly both. There maybe some absorption due to the insulation element. If you have a roof that has a 1:1 difficulty ratio and the activity is greatly delayed, it's for a good reason, maybe bowed decking or a combination of all of the above. Positive static pressure may be playing a part as well.

Start Time Ratios

Average Activity Start time on roof type 2:1

Monsoon Rain Event
About three to five inches of rain per hour
Actual Leak Start Time
About two to three minutes

Heavy rain Event
About an inch of rain per hour
Actual Leak Start Time
About four to five minutes

Moderate rain Event
About three quarters of an inch of rain per hour
Actual Leak Start Time
About five to seven minutes

Average rain Event
About a half inch of rain per hour
Actual Leak Start Time
About seven to fifteen minutes

Light rain Event
About a quarter of an inch of rain per hour
Actual Leak Start Time
About twenty to forty minutes

Mist
About an eight of an inch of rain per hour
Actual Leak Start Time
About forty-five minutes to an hour

If Immediate Activity

If immediate activation of any roof related problem, other sources are always to be taken into consideration and unusual construction designs as a source. Watch out for a roof that may already have a lot of water within, therefore not taking the amount of time usually required for activation. entry point maybe near HVAC or unit, and easily avoiding insulation traveling freely to the exit point.

Slower Activity Time Start

If the leak activity takes longer than 10 minutes, we know that we most likely have a minor Reservoir and/or a small Path of Travel. Could have a small amount of Piggybacking. Possibly a medium to low slope at the deck level.

Longer activity time start

If the leak takes longer than 20 minutes to become active, it could mean that you have a long path of travel. Maybe a large Reservoir. Possibly both. There maybe some absorption due to the insulation element. If you have a roof, that has a 2:1 difficulty ratio and the activity is greatly delayed, that to is for a good reason, maybe bowed decking or a combination of all of the above. Positive static pressure maybe playing a part as well.

Start Time Ratios

Average Activity Start time on roof type 3:1

Monsoon Rain Event
About three to five inches of rain per hour
Actual Leak Start Time
About five minutes

Heavy rain Event
About an inch of rain per hour
Actual Leak Start Time
About ten to fifteen minutes

Moderate rain Event
About three quarters of an inch of rain per hour
Actual Leak Start Time
About fifteen to twenty minutes

Average rain Event
About a half inch of rain per hour

186

Actual Leak Start Time
About thirty minutes

Light rain Event
About a quarter of an inch of rain per hour
Actual Leak Start Time
About an hour

Mist
About an eight of an inch of rain per hour
Actual Leak Start Time
About two to hours

Immediate Activity Time Start

If leak activity was almost immediately after the rain event began, it means it is most likely not roof related. Most likely a problem relating to Other Sources. If roof related, most likely a penetration or opening directly through the roof. Always check all windows, doors and the possibility of condensation building up during high humidity events like the ones that also produce rain.

Slower Activity Time Start

If the leak activity takes about than 30 minutes, we know that we most likely have an above average size Reservoir and/or an above average Path of Travel. Could have a medium to large amounts of Piggybacking, or Secondary reservoirs. Possibly a low to no slope at the deck level. If roof has a lot of dust, dirt and gravel on its surface, time must be allotted to allow for absorption of water to an extent before, it can begin to pond over and entry area and activate a typical roof leak.

Longer activity time start

If the leak takes longer than two hours to become active, it could mean that you have a long path of travel. Maybe a large Reservoir. Most likely both. There maybe some absorption due to the insulation element. If you have a roof that has a 3:1 difficulty ratio, and the activity is greatly delayed, that to is for a good reason, maybe bowed decking or a combination of all of the above. Positive static pressure maybe playing a part as well.

Start Time Ratios

Average Activity Start time on roof type 4:1

Monsoon Rain Event
About three to five inches of rain per hour.
Actual Leak Start Time
About ten minutes.

Heavy rain Event
About an inch of rain per hour.
Actual Leak Start Time
About twenty minutes.

Moderate rain Event
About three quarters of an inch of rain per hour
Actual Leak Start Time
About thirty minutes

Average rain Event
About a half inch of rain per hour
Actual Leak Start Time
About thirty-five to forty-five minutes

Light rain Event
About a quarter of an inch of rain per hour.
Actual Leak Start Time
About an hour and thirty minutes.

Mist
About an eight of an inch of rain per hour.
Actual Leak Start Time
About two to three hours.

Immediate Activity Time Start

If leak activity was almost immediately after the rain event began, means it is absolutely not roof related. Because of this type of Over All Ratio type roof, there will most likely be no roof leak becoming active immediately after rain starts, unless there is earlier saturation as we spoke of before or there is an entry point that has created an opening through the membrane, insulation down into the decking. This would allow water in almost instantaneously.

Slower Activity Time Start

If the leak activity takes longer than 45 minutes, we know that we most likely have a major Reservoir and/or an extensive Path of Travel. Could have large amounts of Piggybacking, and Secondary reservoirs. Possibly low to no slope at the deck level.

Longer activity time start

If the leak takes longer than 3 hours to become active, it could mean that you have a cross lateral circulation path of travel. Maybe a huge Reservoir or Reservoirs, possibly both. Most likely a lot of absorption due to the insulation element. If you have a roof that has a 4:1 difficulty ratio and the activity is greatly delayed, that to is for a good reason, maybe solid, or concrete decking or a combination of all of the above. Positive static pressure maybe playing a part as well.

Residuals from chapter 16

All roofs and roof related problems/roof leaks have an E over E ratio.

The E over E ratio is the measured distance between the entry point and exit point.

An E over E ratio is a difficulty measuring tool used to justify time spent.

An E over E ratio can be parallel, perpendicular or diagonal.

The O.A.R. is to be used to estimate difficulty level in advance before working on new or unfamiliar roofs.

There are four difficulty levels relating to the Over All Ratio.

1:1 O.A.R., Time typically spent, maximum of three hours per two men.
> Difficulty level: Easy

2:1 O.A.R., Time typically spent, no less than three and usually no more than five hours, per two men.
> Difficulty level: Easy to medium difficulty

3:1 O.A.R., Time typically spent no less than three up to eight hours, per two men.
> Difficulty level: Very Difficult

4:1 O.A.R., Time typically spent, five hours, up to what could be two to three days.
> Difficulty level: Extremely Difficult

Chapter 17

Protocols and Processes

This chapter will give you basic direction and time saving methods by following common sense applications as they occur systematically from arriving at the job site to finishing the repair needed to stop the unwanted roof related activity. This chapter is about the proper processes at the proper time.

For example, we do not want to start searching on the roof before we have collected measurements from our actual exit point from within the building.

Leaving the Office

You should receive a work sheet or work order for your customer or several at the beginning of the day. If you have paperwork that corresponds with your work order, make sure that every work order is completely filled out at the end of each job. Always do that before moving on to the next job. Collect signatures if required by your employer.

While at your office/warehouse, have your helper refurbish materials and or replace broken tools for every type of job and corresponding material possibly needed.

Ensure the appearance of your crew is at least acceptable. Keep your work vehicle as clean and organized as possible. When taking photos, its strongly suggested you take a photo of the work order that for that leak call. This separates each job for the person in the office. After you take the photo of the work order, take a photo of the front of the business. After you meet with customers, you will then take four or five photos of the over all roof. Finally, you will take pictures of any roof related problems and repairs made at each location. It does not hurt to take a couple of photos of each roof related problem just in case the image is hard to make out.

Electrical cords, plastic and garden hoses, or you may need to control a roof leak at several locations until repairs can be made. Never borrow these items from the customer. It looks very unprofessional as you should be prepared.

As far as insurance goes, if you own your own company you will be required to have the million dollar plus insurance along with workers compensation, and so on and so forth. Keep this information current, and keep copies of those records with you at all times.

For the rest of us who work for someone else or a roofing company. Insurance requirements are to be covered by your company. You are not to be responsible for any of the insurance costs unless you are a private contractor or self-employed. Either way, have copies that should be supplied to you by your employer in your glove compartment, and keep and eye on keeping them up to date.

It's easy to loose track. Myself drove around for three years on expired tags on my work truck. Never once was I pulled over, someone in my office just happen to check and found we were breaking the law. We did have the new stickers, but failed to put them on.

If paperwork is not available

If you do not have the proper insurance and requirements as requested by customers, corporations and so on. You may be denied access to the work area and/or property and maybe asked to leave until the paperwork issue is cleared up.

If paper work is available

If you do have all required paperwork, you should have no problem accessing the property or the problem area. You will also have access to sensitive areas, just stay within their protocols and rules.

Use GPS for all leak calls

Travel time to the job or customer can be brought in to question, if there are large amounts of mileage and hours charged to the repair. To cut down on wasted time use a GPS device to direct you to the customer's location in the shortest amount of time. A GPS will take you the shortest and quickest route 98% of the time from my own personal experiences.

Do not use the scenic routes. Make sure that the address is correct and complete with a direct phone number to the customer or person meeting you at the location.

If you do

If you do choose to use a GPS, rest assured that as long as you have the correct address, your GPS would take you to most jobs flawlessly and quicker than without.

If you don't

If you do not utilize a GPS, expect to get wrong directions by good intending people. Not everyone who gives you wrong directions is doing it on purpose, either way you can become hopelessly lost and spend a huge amount of time and gas just to get back on track.

Check in with your contact

Always check in with the customer/contact or security and make sure you are seen. Be polite and professional. Note the time of arrival.

If you do

You have a record of your arrival time just in case there is a dispute in a bill that will be sent to your customer.

If you don't

If you do not check in/sign in with your customer or security, they can dispute the bill and will certainly cost your company money. Moreover, it makes you look like a liar when you cannot prove you were some place when you really were there. Again, if there is an accidental fire or chemical accident, security and/or the emergency workers will not be looking for you, because technically, your not there.

Ask to be taken to the roof related item, or problem

Most of the time upon arriving at almost all businesses, they will usually have someone available to show you the location of the alleged roof leak. If you have to wait for someone to become available, be respectful, and patient.

If someone is available to take you to the leak area

If someone is available to take you to the leak area, this is a great opportunity. This ensures you will be less likely to miss additional roof related problems and you can ask questions about the roof related problem.

If someone is not available to take you to the leak location

Its tough walking around looking for something that may no longer be active. Maintenance workers may have removed the bucket or collection vessel, water and mess created by the roof related problem all together and you may be looking for a ghost. Insist on someone who might be available to show you and your helper the actual leak location, it can make a big difference.

Talk to all witnesses to the activity

Part of being seen, is talking to all the witnesses. Your goal is to collect information of all kinds. Get the right information by asking the right questions in the right way. You will deal with maintenance people most of the time in most facilities.

You will also meet people who do not work at that facility but can tell you some information about the roof leak that may make a big difference in finding the correct solution.

Who to talk to

People who are in charge of the company, area or manager of the plant. There are also people who work next to the roof related problem who are more than glad to give you information. Do not interrupt workers who are busy, or ask any personal questions. Every now and then, you will have someone who has worked right behind a roof leak but never noticed that it was active.

Who not to talk to

Every company or business has these employees. They keep these employees hidden away. Do not bother with Drama Mama's/Papa's or people who appear emotionally or mentally disturbed. You need information, but from the right people.

Things to ask and why

Has this roof related problem been active before?

If yes

Possibly a well-established roof leak. Could have been simply over looked or this item may have an extended path of travel.

If not

If not, this could be a sudden or new leak. Leaks don't suddenly appear for no reason, something must have changed on the roof recently or a long term roof leak as developed.

How long has this roof related problem been active?

If for a long time

If activity has been present for years, there is a good chance that this particular roof leak may be a product of Piggy-backing, and or a lengthy path of travel. In all cases it will be something unusual. Multiple layers of insulation/roof or unusual weather events may be a key.

If for a short time

If activity is recent, it could mean the final developing stage of a legitimate roof leak has just completed its final step. It could also mean we have a HVAC unit or non-roof related problem that has become active. It could also mean there has been some recent damage to the roof suddenly.

Has there been any recent work on the rooftop performed lately?

If so

There may have been something unfinished or not covered up properly. Maybe something forgotten by the previous contractor or worker. There may have been some type of accidental entry point made by a visitor who was working or traveling across the roof. Important rule of thumb, anytime you have a roof leak that is near by any HVAC unit or any type of unit, always search around those areas of interest. Most activity is focused around these items, as is most damaged caused accidentally by people. Warning, don't stop searching if something is found. Always completely investigate all search grid areas.

If not

If no one has been working an HVAC/unit lately does not mean a while ago that someone may have inadvertently created an entry point while doing some work and just recently the activity has developed into an active roof related problem. Remember, most roof related problems are man made.

Have you had problems with your sprinkler system before?

If so

Every now and then, you may run into a business that has had problems with their sprinkler system. Very easy to determine. Check the plumbing under the decking at the exit point location and ensure there are no problems.

If not

Even if the customer tells you there are no problems with their sprinkler systems or plumbing, confirm it for them. Sometimes things aren't exactly as they appear.

Eliminate "O.S."

Before you can begin investigating for a roof leak, you must make sure you have a legitimate roof leak by confirming that the activity is coming directly out of the decking, not from a unit, and obviously not produced by sprinkler systems, leaky pipes or steam supply lines, etc.

If activity is directly under a unit, or appears to be coming from the inside parameter of a unit, write down the unit number and take pictures. Many businesses have lettered or numbered units, if they do not; count them out with a good hand drawn map. Confirm true north locations/map with a hand compass.

If able to negotiate Other Source circumstances

Most calls you and your crew will go to will have good access to the roof leak/exit point area. Negotiating around machinery, working employees should not be a problem. If you are able to negotiate around the environment successfully, you should be able to determine whether the water dripping is coming directly out of the decking, in turn identifying a legitimate roof leak. You should also be able to identify any leaking pipes, condensation problems or overhead water heater leaks.

If unable to negotiate Other Source circumstances

There will be times when you are unable to confirm that a roof related problem might be connected to other sources. Expect once in a while not being physically able to get to the level of the ceiling whatever that height may be. Utilize your zoom on your camera and take pictures if possible.

If its actively leaking check the temperature of the water dripping out of your exit point to see if the water is cooler than normal room temperature, there maybe an HVAC issue, or freezer problem. Truth is, if you cannot get a ladder inside or a high lift, you cannot be held responsible for a mis-diagnosis. The sad part is, it may simply be a plumbing issue that may only need to physically see it.

If you do not have a way, to see completely what is going on, or unable to inspect the required components that are direct or indirect variables to any roof related problem, you are driving blind from the beginning. Tell your customer this and get their help solving it. You would be surprised how much help they are willing to give you. You really do need this information.

Secure accurate measurements of the exit point for your Dual Point Positioning

Measurements from a landmark are okay if you have a small building, but a measuring wheel is recommended. If you do not have a measuring wheel, you will have to measure it by stepping it off. Dual point positioning measurements are to be from at least two known outside walls centered in directly under an active exit point.

Make sure that your helper and yourself collect separate measurements. Do not share them. It's necessary and it could make a big difference in your success rate. Do not forget that the water you see dripping off an I-beam may only be where the water has traveled from an exit point, after it came out of the decking 8 feet further away than it appears. You have to get close enough to see the actual highest point of the water as it is inside the building until it is definitively identified at its exact position. Remember, all the laps of decking will be lying on beams of some sort and will be hidden away from easy view.

If activity is under and with in the boundaries of a unit, go to that unit on the rooftop and look for the problem. If you do find a missing access door or a simple problem you can take care of, just do it. Replace tech screws voids, and some minor caulking is allowed. Take before, after and finish pictures. Check out with the customer, you're done. If you find no obvious problems with the unit, go back down and continue with the next step.

If you don't

If by chance, you cannot secure complete and accurate measurements of the unwanted activity, your chances of success immediately drops like a rock. If you are unable to navigate around large objects, get as close as you can. If possible, use Sound resonance.

If you do

If you are able to collect proper measurements, there will be a lot less guesswork and less worry. These measurements make your investigation solid and surer.

Check the slope of the decking with a level

Collect this information at the very area where the exit point is active.

If you can collect this information

It will show you where the path of travel is coming from. Whatever the slope direction is, you always search uphill or opposite of that slope.

If you cannot collect this information

You will not be able to determine the direction of the path of travel.

Sometimes you may run into a job where the ceiling is excessively high to reach. You may only be able to see the decking and not have access to a lift. You can utilize a digital or laser measuring device. Simply put on the floor-facing straight up, collect measurements the length of the problem area. Move the measuring device to the next section of decking, collect another measurement. Compare the two. There may only be a small different in the measurements, but possibly enough to show you the slope. Under some circumstances, you may have to miss this critical step.

Collect temperature, time, rate and amount information

If the leak is active, utilize a well-marked vessel preferably clear plastic or glass, and collect the water out-put per one-minute intervals, directly under the leak. Do not forget to test the water for temperature. Most cell phones have stopwatches. Make note of the type of rain event that is associated with this particular roof leak.

This information will confirm later if you have successfully stopped the roof leak. That can only happen if the two measurements are made during the same rain event. In other words, it the rain stops while your on the roof, it doesn't matter about getting a secondary measurements because the amount of water from the rain event has dwindled down, and so will your time, rate and amount measurements.

When the rain stops or the rate of the rain diminishes, you can get false positive readings, making you believe that you must have stopped it, because the rate and the amount of water has slowed down.

You can also use disposable clear plastic cups and at the end of one minute simply mark with a fine tip permanent marker the amount on the side of the plastic cup at the water line. Set cup aside somewhere safe as not to wipe off your mark.

If you do

This can give you absolute time, rate and amount information. This will quickly confirm whether you have successfully found the offending entry point.

You will not be able to compare the two different time, rate and amount measurements to determine if you have successfully secured the proper location/entry point.

Remove all ladders and debris that you and your crew utilized and create

Do not clog up walkways with ladders or extension cords at any business during your investigation. This costs them money. It's your job to save them money, this is a negative process. Sometimes the customer may ask you to throw away old or wet ceiling tiles for them, just do it. Place all debris in plastic bags and dispose of properly.

If you do

If you do clean up your mess created by your crew, the customer will be grateful. Besides, you are being paid to work anyway. It makes no sense if have to pay someone else to clean up your mess.

If you don't

If you do clog your customers work area with ladders/extension cords, it can really interfere with their production. This slows down their cash flow. If you and your crew make a mess with wet damaged ceiling tiles without cleaning up the mess, you may not be asked to come back out.

Complete Dual Point Positioning on the roof

The proper steps needed to complete Dual Point Positioning are, collect measurements of the exit point. Also required is the direction of the decking. Finally, a measurement of the slope of the metal decking, and true north markers.

Whether you circle the very exit point or mark it with an X on the surface of the roof, make sure that measurements are an accurate reading from down stairs to up stairs. Some people write the date, time and year as reference information for future endeavors.

If you don't

Not writing down this information on the roof surface can really make life difficult. If you do not identify this specific location, it can drive you crazy, and it's a big waste of time if not done.

If you do

Being able to reference this information when needed is the reason we write it down on the roof. This way your helper isn't walking around asking you repeatedly where the exit point is.

Create a Search Grid

All search grids are relate to the type of roof you are dealing with. If you have a one layer EPDM roof you will dictate you search area on a Over all ratio of 1:1 which will be the most simple and quickest search area. If you have a roof with a concrete deck, multiple layers of insulation or maybe two roofs, you difficulty rating or Over all ratio will be 4:1 which will include a larger majority of the roof. This prevents us from searching too much which wastes time, or not searching enough which does not solve the problem and may warrant a repeat call.

If you do

You can rest assured that you will most likely find something positive an constructive. Matter of fact you may find many things such as failed detail, or other developing but not active roof related problems.

If you don't

Expect to miss some something, somewhere guaranteed!

Inspect the roof within the search area

Areas of interest during a roof inspection are; Pathways, Walk ways, around all penetrations and units. Areas of high traffic tend to have more deficiencies than normal, due to natural and man made intervention/action.

Make sure you search out every square inch of the search area from different views and angles. You are looking for, cuts, holes even slices and punctures, bullet holes. Open laps, failed flashing or evidence left behind from something or anything.

An example would be if you would find an access door or a piece of metal just lying on the roof. Chances are there may be an entry point between the unit and that access panel. There is always a possibility that the wind may have rolled it around across the roof surface, creating many entry points.

In addition, the leak may not have become active until after some work was done to the unit. After repair was made and access panel was replaced properly, the customer could request a water test or request that you come back out to confirm the unwanted activity has ceased.

Proper Inspections

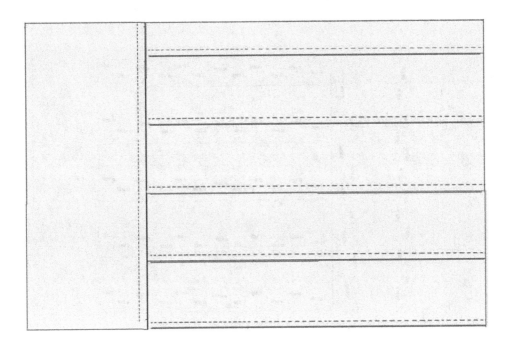

Above we have a typical rubber membrane cartoon drawing of a roof. Notice the laps are bar-in-seam and of, course no safeties or T-joint protection. How would you walk the roof? Most walk around until we find something good.

A good tech walks the roof along laps, and divides the roof up into sections. This prevents missing the all-important entry point.

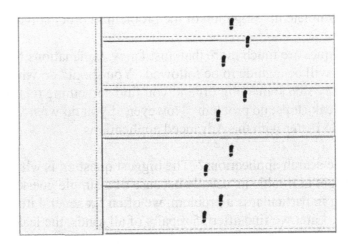

Above the careless movement of the unskilled tech. Unintentionally missing up to 90% of the roof surface. Some repair people even I have actually stood directly on the entry point and was unable to see or find it. In some cases that instituted a return call. Always check exactly where you are standing first before searching onward.

Below is the proper search technique.

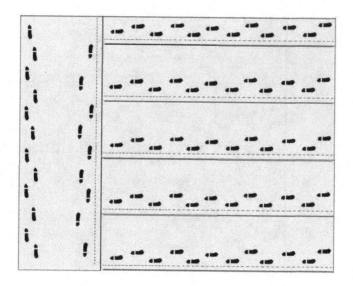

If you have ever seen someone working in a body shop. Typically, they eliminate each section before they move on to something else. For instance, they may start with the front fender. After work on the fender has been completed, and it is satisfactory to the worker, he or she will move on to the hood, or maybe on to the door.

The reasoning for this is to have a high quality outcome by systematically eliminating all imperfections per area. Like a good detective, you have to look at every square inch and every square foot, to have a complete investigation of the problem in order solve it.

Advanced search techniques are much more than just fancy explanations for process that have been improved on, they will be a guide to be followed. You should do what works for you, for instance if you just simply step something off and you find something relatively close on the roof, you fix it and the leak stops, no problem. However, if you do what you usually do and it nets nothing, you may do better with the Advanced applications.

How would you advance search applications? The biggest question is what information do you really need? When we get in trouble its usually because of a simple guess. Rather than knowing for a fact that something in particular is a problem, we often fix several items in a particular area as not to miss anything. Later we find after 15 repairs of all kinds, the leak persists.

Other proper inspections

Lets talk about the hand level and its uses. A small hand level can tell us so much about the state of the leak/activity. If you look up at the bottom side of a building and you see metal decking, can you just how level that decking is? Can you tell if it has a slope or not? On the roof over top of that same deck may be distorted especially due to maybe a tapered system. Matter of fact the decking may slope east to west and the insulation may slope north to south. Advance search techniques are only taking advantage of every tool available to you which means you have to put together the two in Perpendicular and parallel strategies.

If you are having a hard time with a roof leak and you cannot reach the decking from the bottom side, arrange a lift of some sort. Physically see for yourself which way the water is coming from and going to and make a note. Hand levels work on the roof as well, ball barrings are more fun. Ping-Pong balls, kick balls or even tennis balls can tell you the fall of the roof in general if thrown up hill and allowed to roll back toward the pitcher. Again that may only be an optical illusion and not the actual slope of the decking.

When ever possible, use the hand level on the bottom side of the decking and get an accurate reading. It may take you in the opposite direction away from the areas and locations where others have failed. Like following the money, or scent you have to follow the slope.

In some cases you will not be allowed or have access to a certain areas to check how level or what type of slope there might be associated with the decking in question. Unfortunately you will have to deal with the roof related activity you have. When this does happen a fail safe is to inspect the entire length of the hard path of travel. Again, an advanced technique is going the extra mile.

Measuring wheels are so very important when it comes to large buildings, warehouses or any open area with a lot of space. We all love to just walk an area off and simply just remember the measurements and for some reason we ask our helpers what measurements they collected? Even though, very rarely are people exactly the same height, ten steps for you may be a little further than my ten steps.

Don't go by other peoples measurements. Always secure your own. If in doubt or the area is large/makes no sense, use a measuring wheel and double check yourself. One helper would get twelve steps for every ten of mine. So for twenty steps he would have about twenty four steps. When his measurement was thirty one steps and I had thirty, I knew one of us had miscounted. Stop what your doing, get new measurements. It really is worth it. You will get use to the ratio between you and your helper and when the ratio doesn't sound right, you'll know.

Touchy Feely is something we touched on earlier. Many repairman only look at the roof and if they don't see anything serious or important and they move on with their investigation. Please don't be that guy. It is easy to see flashing that looks well attached and by just simply touching it slightly, it could just fall off the wall. Looks are very deceiving. One of the main reasons of my success is that I pulled and pushed, yanked on everything on the roof that was nailed down or not. By constantly performing this task it has lead me to large and surprising finds. From small pin holes, to long fine razor cut slices. Again, just looking at the same area with the naked eye, everything looked just fine until it was touched. Spread the rubber apart, open those units and look in there and see what is going on inside if need be. Wear gloves as much as possible.

Digital thermometers are an advanced tool that serves a purpose when an HVAC unit or steam pipe that maybe leaking needs to be confirmed. A simple vessel is required under the activity, after a few minutes of collection depending on the rate, take a reading and write it down.

Compare that temperature to the outside temperature. Temps really warm, probably steam pipe if one is present. Temp is colder than outside temperature, probably HVAC related. If temperature is same as outside, then probably roof related.

Pointer laser is pretty helpful because it gives your customer a way to communicate a location they cannot reach. Often commercial and industrial building are two and three stories high. You can ask a customer, where the leaks is located at and the best they can do is give you a general point in a general location. A laser pointer can allow then to point to a specific rib, flute or beam. There maybe one single screw hole where water dripped out of that is in the middle of 20 others. Have one handy, the customer will appreciate it.

Compass is an old fashion thing but almost everyone has them on their smart phones. A compass is simply a quick way to get you situated so you can find you way from one location to another. In essence you are pinging one spot with a measurement, going on the roof and pinging the same spot with the help of the directions in relation to your measurements. You do not need one on every job. They can save you a lot of head ache and may save you from going to the wrong end of the building by accident. When it comes to an important job, or a repeat problematic situation don't hesitate to pull out all the stops. Who knows, maybe the reason the leak wasn't found is because the design of the building was confusing which caused people to go to the wrong location over and over again. This is just another tool to be sure of yourself.

Screw drivers with adjustable bits are so handy because the allow us access to places most don't get to see. Sometimes we just need to see the decking only to know if there is either water in the channels, or if there are rocks and dirt or what ever. It doesn't matter the reason for the access we sometimes have to have it.

Dog boxes are a good source to see down to the deck. Often they have slide off tops and they slide off. Eventually they are fastened permanently with mechanical fasteners. You will need a screw driver. Because so many people access these things who knows what you will need. That's why we need multi-tipped bits. HVAC units can also be good access areas to see the decking or areas in between depending on the type of unit. Don't waste time with extension cords unless absolutely necessary. This is only intended an designed for a quick look only and to re-fasten any loose panels or dog box lids. Also, if you have other pipe collars or even clamps, you can also tighten them down as well.

What would be the best advanced search technique you could get? Well, one good hint is to always check around units first. Anytime you have a roof leak running parallel to or from an HVAC unit, go to the unit and check it out. We are not picking on anyone, it just so happens accidents really do happen. That's why its important to ask if anyone has serviced their HVAC units recently or changed out filters. Don't spend hours around the units, just a quick look and see.

No proper inspection

If you do not comb the roof surface completely, chances are you will miss quite a bit. Moving too fast, glancing and not physically inspecting the roof surface can kill your success rate, reputation and confidence. Even if an entry point has been discovered, do not stop there. Keep searching, just in case there are more.

Conduct a Trough Search

Within your search grid look the roof over for obvious wet or dry but damaged insulation called Troughing. Troughing feels soft and spongy when walked on.

Quickest way to find Troughing is to look for ponding. If dirty looking or stained ponded areas are near, perpendicular or parallel from your exit point, that is an immediate area of interest.

On ballasted or graveled roofs, the easiest way to search for Troughing is to look for dirty graveled areas. Areas of gravel that appear to be in lower ponded areas due to high water marks. All ponding will have watermarks, Troughing will have watermarks but is often dirty or stain as to their appearance on many occasions.

If no Troughing on roof

There will be times when there will be no troughing. If water that has entered into the system and did not make contact with insulation there will be little to no Troughing. If the roof related problem is brand new, troughing will not be have a chance to develop.

If extensive Troughing on roof

Every once in a while you may run into a roof that is covered with troughing. The entire roof maybe damaged due age, re-skinning activity. Disregard any Trough searching, do not waste the time. It will only lead you to false positives. It maybe possible to find a softer than usual spot to investigate, but very unlikely.

Utilize Perpendicular and Parallel Strategies

Take into consideration the slope of the deck, type of insulation and how many layers with the options of a path of travel/Piggy-Backing will dictate the size and scope of your search grid in relation to the exit point/roof leak and the type of materials that make up the roof.

Utilizing Perpendicular and Parallel Strategies

Your odds are greatly increased if you take into consideration all the variables such as insulation, slopes and amounts in searching and solving a roof related problems.

Not Utilizing Perpendicular and Parallel Strategies

Will result in not thoroughly searching enough area for possible entry points. Remember, repeat only means investigation didn't go far enough.

If early morning or after a rain, inspect for Internal Thermal Identification

If your visit happens to come after a rain event ends or just when the rain stops, you may be able to depend on, I.T.I., to give you some help. This is also true for early morning when the dew is drying up. The last areas to completely dry up on the roof usually are connected to the roof leak/roof related problem in most cases.

Avoid utilizing propane tanks to initiate I.T.I., unless the operator has had extensive training with propane torches and that particular roof material. Never use propane torches on any heat-weld system.

If roof has moisture within the system

If there is moisture within the system, you may be able to identify entry points under the conditions of morning dew, and after a rain event.

If roof has no moisture within the system

If there is no moisture within the system, you will not get a positive indicator in the form of water seeping back out of entry points.

Check all Curbs/Penetrations

Inspect all Penetrations and units within and even close to the search area, as 72% of all entry points will be located around these items.

What to check

When ever you are trying to cancel out an item from your list of possible sources that could be causing a roof related problem, check the entire unit. Ventilation ductwork can pull in water from outside. Around the parameter of any unit/HVAC unit, penetration is probably the most important areas to check out on the roof.

Utilize Sound Resonance if you cannot identify any areas around a unit that maybe pulling water in with outside air, mimicking a roof leak.

What not to check

Stay away from large units that are not even close to your work area. Some guys waste time just walking around looking at stuff. Do not do that. If there are unusual landmarks, buildings or heater house applications that are not or could not be part of the problem, stay away from them. Spend your time wisely.

Secure Entry point(s) and make repairs

Make permanent repairs if possible. Make sure you and your helper apply the same type of materials per roof and respective manufacturer per repair. This includes re-attaching access doors to units, re-attaching coping metal and caulking around loose fitting hardware such as rain skirts, caps, etc.

How to secure

Once you find an entry point it becomes secured when, marked with chalk and photographed.

How not to secure

Not marking all roof related problems is a big mistake. It is so easy to just walk away when there are so many other things going on. Always mark every last thing and photo graph it.

Clear the roof of any other deficiencies and entry points

While your helper is making the actual repair, clear the roof of, loose metal flashings, access doors, antennas not properly secured. Loose or missing fasteners around HVAC units and make sure all drains are open and flowing as they should be. These very small and quick items make a roof function properly, make sure they are working as they should, take pictures and inform the customer of the condition of their roof.

If no new deficiencies are found

Make a note. No other repairs are needed.

If new deficiencies are found

Make a list of locations and count of how many. Make repairs at all entry points, remove debris from drains, scuppers and/or replace missing fasteners at units/penetrations. Take before and after photos.

If raining, temp entry points

Collect time, rate and amount measurements from the exit point location. If you have made the proper repair, the leak's rate and amount should diminish within your one-minute interval cycles. If it were raining while on the roof before you made the temp and after you have collected your second measurement and they are less, success.

You have cut off the source to a roof leak and it's been confirmed scientifically. There will be no bells, whistles or parades but you know you have done a great job when you confirm it. Not only did you find the entry point but also you were able to give the customer what they needed, relief, peace of mind confidence in your work. At least some relief until permanent repairs can be made.

If temps cannot be made

Sometimes temps will not take because of the type of material. The lap sealant may not be compatible enough to ensure a good watertight seal. If this does happen, hang up plastic and divert water into a vessel that can be handled by all that work around the area. Do not set up a 55-gallon barrel under a small roof leak with two elderly secretaries left to deal with removing the accumulating water. This does not count against a roof repair personnel.

If temps can be made

If your lap sealant is compatible enough to make solid temps, make sure that you count every one. You may come back, make two permanent repairs on the next dry day, and not remember how many temps you made. If possible, make a small map of the general areas if many temps are required and you have a lot of surface to cover.

If high humidity while making Permanent Repairs

If you are lucky enough to get to a repair down while the rain has let up long enough to make a permanent repair, by all means do so. Consider the dew point and humidity rates. The higher they are, the more moisture between your patch and surface membrane. If needed, utilize a heat gun to completely dry these applicable materials properly and completely.

If you can

If you can dry out this material completely or at least enough to make a permanent repair, you can save yourself another trip, especially if out of town.

If you can't

If you cannot make a permanent repair during your service call, you will have to make a return visit, which is another charge for the customer.

Check out with the customer

If repairs or temps have been made and you have gone over cause and effect scenarios or possible explanations and you bid your farewells, check out with Security or any governing entities that maybe responsible for your well being.

If you do

If you do check out with your customer, there can be very little dispute as your departure time goes. If the customer does witness you leaving the premises, they cannot dispute the departure time or the bill.

If you don't

If you do not check out with the customer, they can and in some cases go out of their way to dispute your departure time. This can cost you and your company valuable time and money.

What happens when a plan does not come together? What if? That is a big question in its self. What happens when you hit barriers? Typically, there are so many things that can give us false positives and false hope, and there are things that can lead us to the source. In other words, if something doesn't present its self at first, that's because there are mitigating factors that make it unique or unusual in the world of roof repairs.

If and when you return

If and when you come back, it will only be for a few of reasons. One reason, a good reason is that you were forced to make a temp due to a previous investigation because of an impending rain event.

You could have made temps and the activity may have stopped at most locations, except one or two. There for you maybe returning to continue your investigation.

Finally, your reason for coming back may be that you need to conduct a controlled water test to confirm a suspicion that you may be dealing with, penetration or cracked drainpipe, something of that nature.

You may have done a bang up job, stopped the leak, and may be called back either for a new roof leak or maybe some maintenance work. If you're doing maintenance work something secondary to that effect, then do so. For the rest of us that have to come back because the leak may have been active beyond our repair, or reactivated or you are simply not sure about the entry point location, this is what you must do. Start over from the beginning. Confirm all previous measurements and redefine your boundaries for your search area or areas. If the leak is active after repairs, whether temporary or permanent, consider residual drainage covered in Chapter 20.

When you return

Go over search area again and completely

Second time around will usually go quicker/faster. Sometimes you can see items that weren't so obvious on your previous visit. The reason for this is simply because when we usually return it will be on a dry day with no rain.

Collect new Dual point positioning measurements and do not waste time questioning everyone about the leak again. Just make it short and sweet. You should already have good information, but just in case you missed something important, remember you are starting all over as if it's a new investigation, do ask if anything has changed. If there has been a change in the activity such as the amount or location, collect new measurements as if its a new leak call and compare the two.

Internal Thermal Identification

If you do have a problem roof that, few have had success with. Lets say you do get to come back to continue your investigation. Try to schedule it for early morning. I.T.I. can help direct us straight to the entry point very quickly, if given the chance.

Conduct a Trough search

Anytime that a repair crew comes back to a repeat leak, you must always conduct a trough search. If raining during your original visit, there may have been too much of a distraction while in a typical rain event to identify Troughing.

Sometimes, the second time around may drag out information that was unseen or over looked previously under calmer conditions.

Utilize a Stethoscope for Sound Resonance

If other processes have failed, you should utilize Sound Resonance. You will be listening for muffled or clear sound indicators. The more muffled, the more saturated our insulation will be. The clearer or crisp the sound wave traveling through the insulation is, the drier it is.

Conduct a Water Test with Time Differentials

If no entry points can be secured, a Water test with time differentials may be in order. Always get permission to utilize a water test as they do take time and money. However, the savings of having someone come out every time it rains with the same effect is much more expensive. Follow the levels properly starting at your lowest point and allowing enough time between saturating locations before you move on. Do not soak down a large area. Typically, ten by ten foot or three meter areas are plenty. If you activate a roof leak in an area that you soaked that is 100 foot square, you still have only narrowed it down to a large area to search out. Water testing is designed to minimize false positives by activating a roof related problem within a certain time frame. Always make sure there is nothing of any value under the leak area that can be damaged during the water test.

If needed Utilize Surgical Intervention

As a last case scenario, use surgical intervention and look for evidence such as reservoirs, paths of travel or damaged materials like insulation or rusted decking

These are the initial steps to complete a typical and extreme roof repair call. The most important thing is to not get discourage and never give up.

Residuals from chapter 18

Be prepared for long distance travel, work orders and materials with a good helper.

Take pictures of the work order, front of the building and always check in with the customer.

Meet with the customer, be professional.

Identify the problem whether it is roof related or not, eliminate the possibility of O.S.

Collect proper measurements with dual point positioning, if building is large utilize a measuring wheel. I recommend utilizing a measuring wheel on every call unless the building is small like a drive-thru or mini mart. Collection of measurements are required by you and your helper.

Collect levelness of decking if possible and look for your path of travel.

Transfer measurements to the roof.

Decide on the size of the search grid on the type of roof you have. Whether it is a 1:1 or 4:1 Over all ratio.

Utilize the proper search techniques within the search areas and add all units and penetrations near by these search areas even if they are 10 feet away from the exit point.

Secure entry points. Make repairs and clear the roof of any other roof related problems near by. Never stop the investigation after finding an entry point or even two or three. Clear the entire area.

If permanent repairs cannot be made, make temps and repair them on a return call. Also quickly clear the roof in case you missed something small.

If leak is active even after you have made repairs, begin your investigation over or get permission to conduct a water test. You may have to activate the roof leak to track the activity with surgical intervention.

Water testing with time differentials with separate a window issue from HVAC problem and will definitely tell you if you do not have a roof related problem.

Chapter 18

Temps

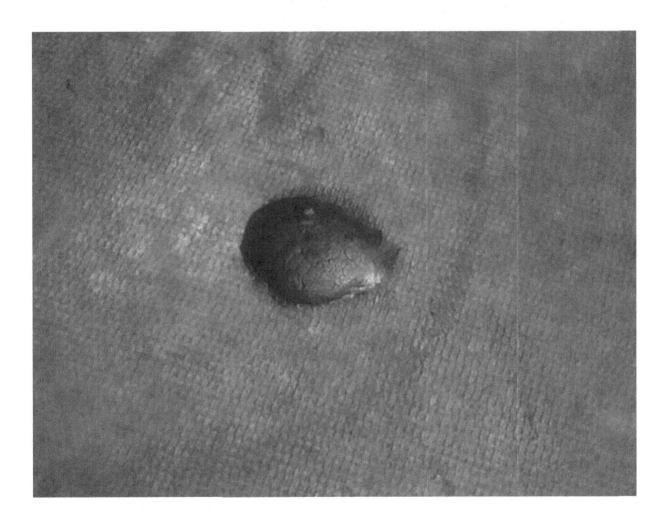

    Let us talk about temps and what they mean for the Repair Specialist. The picture above is a temp put on during the rain onto a reinforced rubber membrane roof.

Temps should always be applied in a chocolate drop shape or dollop. This way you have maximum amount of coverage over the entry point. It is so very important to put enough that it will last a long time and withstand the pressure from within the building and roof.

This is where static positive pressure comes in and can definitely wreck a temp. Sometimes we can find multiple entry points. The largest so far for myself was about 115 temps. This was spread out of a very large area. It did stop the water from coming in but this of course is temporary.

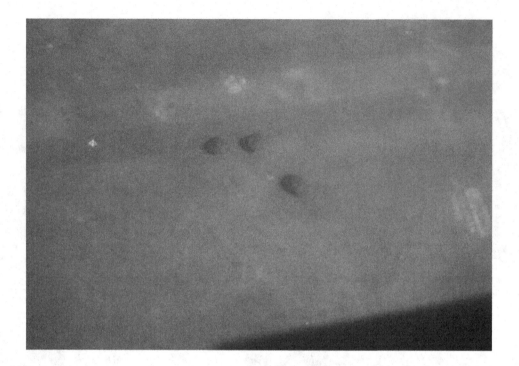

Notice the chocolate drop shape of these three puncture covered temps. The dirtier the membrane, the more difficult it is for the lap sealant to adhere. Temps should always be applied first with the smallest amount of lap sealant and scrubbed in with your fingertips until it adheres to the membrane. All you are trying to do is prime the membrane or surface, and then you apply a dollop of lap sealant over the primed entry point.

Anytime the lap sealant balls up and does not stick, it's because you are using too much or the surface is too dirty or both. Keep rubbing in the lap sealant in very small amounts, it will stick.

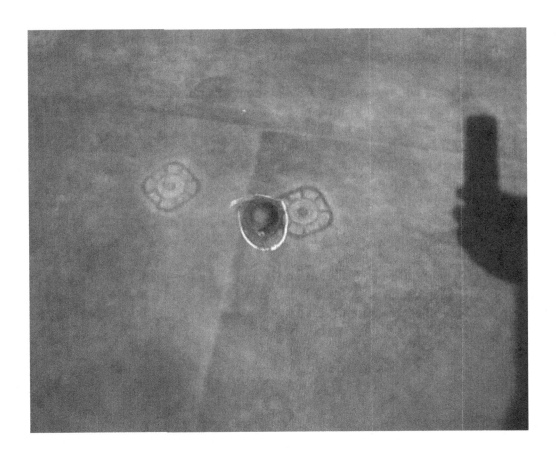

In the picture above, we have a temp that is ready to pop because of the pressure.

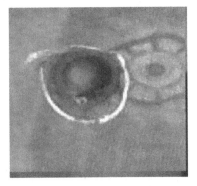

While making permanent repairs during this particular call we had six temps pop like balloons but the others held up very well. They inflated, then hardened up.

Do not use other caulks to apply temps other than lap sealant. This will often allow oils and chemicals to contaminate/infect the surface of the roof.

We never remove the temps when we go back to make a permanent repair unless they are inflated or over sized. Just in case there is a problem with the patch, or chemical application or maybe even a day of high humidity and we were not aware of it, that temp is our insurance policy. If the temp is sticking up a little, smash it flat, wash and glue as usual and patch.

Many roofing companies will not want me to talk about this but in some or even many cases these are the facts. We as prevention specialists not only stop a problem for today but stop problems from coming back tomorrow, fair enough?

Every now and then we will fin what we call a divot. Divots or even scrapes are not entirely through the membrane of the roof, but as time goes by they will open up and create a roof related problem. Myself have been yelled at by an asshole boss who told me he did not want me to do that because that cuts into his money. In other words, he doesn't mind if my reputation suffered from not doing my job as long as he made a sale. I quit!

Just because you see a dollop on the roof surface it could be a forgotten temp but more than that, if you went behind a responsible repairman like myself, you will find where I was looking out for my customers best interests rather than a greedy business owner who wants to buy his wife a new fancy car for her birthday at the cost of my reputation.

When you see something suspicious, add a dollop as a buffer or bumper to protect the customer or even yourself from getting a call on Christmas day away from your family. Your boss or business owner, does not care about you, your reputation or that customer. Only the money they can take from them and you! That's been true at every company I have ever worked at.

Also, a temp can be a small a mount of primer scrubbed through water and lap sealant applied on top. Circumstances require unusual solutions. Experiment and see what works for different applications. Not all the answers are here, the possibilities are endless and they are out there with you on the job site.

Residuals from chapter 18

If a permanent repair cannot be made due to, time restraints or weather conditions always apply some type of a temp regardless of the materials on hand as your job is to bring relief to the customer.

Always utilize lap sealant on EPDM Roofs. Roof Cement on Built-Up.

Never use construction caulk, water block to make a temp.

Never use roof cement on rubber roofs, or use lap sealant on Built-up roofs. However, you are the master of your own destiny, if you are with your back against the wall, and you have no lap sealant to utilize on a rubber roof, by all means utilize roof cement cotton or nylon membrane. When you come back, cut out all the area touched by the roof cement. This is probably not recommended by roofing material producing companies and frankly I don't give a damn. They are not the one who may be 500 miles from home, with no materials with a customer who is on the verge of loosing every thing just because of some office person saying, "No you can't do that because I say so." Do what you need to do to save the customer. That's your job, not satisfying some faceless office person who does understand your customer needs.

When applying a temp, always apply a very tiny amount to prime the entry point area, then apply the covering temporary patch in the form of lap sealant. Mark as temp.

When apply a Dollop as a buffer or bumper as a preventative measure, do not rub it in or smooth it out. Do not mark as temp.

Use a healthy amount or dollop size amount on all entry points in case pressure inside the building pushes air into the lap sealant, this prevents popping or reopening of the entry point.

Do not use tape to make a temp <u>ever</u>.

Utilizing Lap Sealant (Dollop) over scuffs and scrapes is considered preventative maintenance.

Temps should not be left alone for more than a week. Make permanent repairs as soon as possible. Temps are that, temporary.

Chapter 19

Residual Drainage

   One sure way to get a roofing company or repair person in trouble is to have residual drainage and not being able to identify it. Most customers think that water will drain out of the affected area until it's empty and no more, but for the real world of roof related problems, that is not always the case.

Even though the entry point has been found and properly repaired, it can reactivate under the right circumstances making the repairman/woman technically, into a liar. Residual drainage is a short-lived event in most cases, but it can cause long-term problems with our reputations and relationships with our customers if not properly addressed in advance. The last thing we need is for the customer to doubt our ability or judge our ability on something we have no control over like residual drainage. Understanding the process of residual drainage and being able to explain it to our customers is paramount like all other processes that go on at the roof level.

Besides customers don't get angry when they realize that the unwanted activity is only a natural process as the leak wraps up, and it will not leak again once the natural order of the roof leak process completes its task. Definitely, but not always, residual drainage is part of that task during some circumstances. A good thing about residual drainage is, after it occurs its becomes very predictable.

Reactivation of any roof leak that has just been repaired usually means the repairman did not fix the problem from the customers point of view, but as long as you warn them of the possibility they usually wait it out patiently with no argument and you will not get unnecessary blame. Even better than that, because you were able to tell the customer how and when it may reactivate and it actually does, and does run its natural course, to the customer you'll be brilliant and they will want you back on future calls.

Understanding how residual drainage is understanding components like the amount of water that was been left behind within the flutes of the decking after the leak has become inactive. Do not forget about the water inside the insulation or around the edges of the insulation and how far the path of travel might be. Remember that a lot of water can lie within the parameters of the actual roof but not leak a drop.

Before you leave the customer and the water has stopped from your initial repair, you have to let them know about the fact that there is water trapped within the system and that it may drain out under the right circumstances. It's always best to tell every customer these facts during every call even though it may happen once out of every 20 leak calls.

Some customers demand facts and it is your job to tell them the facts but how do you predict something you cannot see with the naked eye. Let us look at common and certain facts concerning the process of residual drainage also known as "Secondary or Ghost leaks." What activates these secondary leaks will usually be one of or a combination of; natural drainage/gravity, expansion/pressure or heat elements.

Imagine making a repair in the rain, and you know you have found the entry point and stopped the activity with a good and solid temp. The next day, for no reason just before the warmest part of the day the leak becomes active. Nothing has changed on the roof since your visit, the difference is the sunshine, but some how it's leaking, again!

It wasn't leaking this morning but now after lunch it began leaking for no reason. There is a reason, a scalding hot reason. Thermal heating from the sun can be warm to dangerously hot within the roof from water stored within the system in the form of reservoirs. Actually, from my own witness accounts, first and second-degree burns happen for those without gloves if they open up the roof with pockets of water and are not careful. You can step on a blister and bust it on a built-up roof and it can spray water into some poor unsuspecting persons eyes. It happens more than you would think, and only takes a second. Always be weary about scalding hot water in a roof system. Matter of fact on a sunny summer day you can see temperatures on the roof surface reach 140 degrees Fahrenheit or better. Believe it or not, it can be much warmer within the system, especially if there is a facility that keeps a warmer than average temperature inside the building.

Residual drainage can happen due to weight from water during the next rain or two and possibly three, seems like it will never stop leaking. Even though there is no new or fresh water being fed into the roof membrane or system that is causing reactivation, it can pretend or act just like the same actual roof leak that was repaired previously, but there is a specific change that makes all the difference. The change, a lot less activity. We can measure this and confirm residual activity.

Luckily these types of Ghost leaks are short lived. This natural draining process will repeat time and time again, each time it rains until the reservoirs, path of travel completely drain out and down enough for the leak to become inactive. The weight on the roof over all of even a quarter of an inch is a lot of weight spread out over the length and width of the surface of the roof. This weight will push out what remains inside if the reservoirs have drain down to the lowest point. And, again residual drainage happens when the sun warms up a very saturated roof, expanding water inside which will push out the excessive water.

Again, this is not going to happen during every roof leak call. It does happen and can catch you off guard if you're not expecting the possibility. Try to remember that residual drainage events happen with "well established" or "long active life" roof leaks, and are uncommon for brand new roofs. The reason for that is that is takes time for the water to develop a larger Reservoir and Path of travel.

One thing you can depend on is your measurements. You should measure the amount of water leaking out with a measuring type cup or bowl and measure the time, that way you have an accurate account of the activity such as rate and amount. No matter what you measure, you are looking for dramatically less water than in earlier measurements. These earlier measurements are from the initial leak call. If it is the same amount leaking in the same amount of time, then you have an entry point to find. If it is dramatically less, residual drainage.

Customers expect a certain amount of satisfaction and time from you and you must provide that service as requested anyway. This is much better then guesstimating on uncertain information. You will always measure the amount of water against 60-second intervals with a stopwatch. Besides there is nothing wrong with confirming your findings. This is real science use it!

Who knows, someone might have come up after you and dropped something at that location. We will not know until we clear the roof and any other possibility that may have created a secondary problem. Because water has a memory, any new entry point close to an old roof leak will always feed right back into the established pathway. There is no exception to that rule ever.

Another strange and even rarer occurrence of residual drainage can happen where we will least suspect it is when roof freezes up. Some conditions that freeze a roof solid happen once or twice a year during the wintertime.

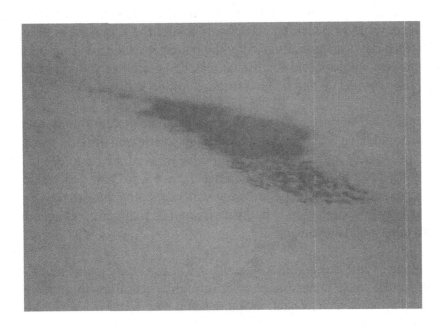

This picture above shows a roof that is frozen solid except for a low-lying area that had water under the ice. This shows us a huge loss of R-factor or transference of heat. This happens when heat travels through wet insulation from the bottom up and melts the ice.

When we were called out to this roof above, it was leaking even though the outside temperature was twelve degrees Fahrenheit. That's an automatic red flag. Technically, it's too cold for roofs to leak. Utilizing I.T.I., we discovered the area above as probably the main area or source of the roof leak. We moved snow, ice and water and found several entry points. This took a while and in the process as the sun went down and the temperature dropped substantially the activity also stopped. The temperature dropped enough to deactivate the leaking inside. We were convinced that we slowed or stopped the leaking with out temps. By the end of the day, we were beat up, frozen and frustrated. It's a lot of work shoveling, pushing and patching under those extreme conditions.

The next day it warmed up in the afternoon and the area we worked on had been cleaned off exposing the membrane to the warm sunshine. The sun heated the roof and the leak activity went crazy! They called us back and told us to get our asses out there or else. We did rush out there only to find three to four inches of standing water on the affected area. We shoveled out a drainage ditch to the roof conductors and applied water pumps. The leak only got worst.

Finally, we found an entry point, then another and another. We also found out later that we were causing the newer entry points with our shovels. That hurt, a lot. I ordered everyone to stop, so we patched what we could and temped the rest. Again toward the end of the day the leak stopped as the temperature dropped. I informed the customer it may be residual drainage or water in the system and we should let it drain out completely first before we proceed with a plan b, or c.

Not surprised that for the next three days it would leak when the sun warmed up the roof in the warmest part of the day and stop leaking completely at night. I asked the manager to check if the water amount per each day was less. Every day the manager called and reported that the water amount had become less and less, and finally the leak had completely stopped. We were very happy because it also warmed up and began raining a lot, no leaks.

If we made the repairs and stepped back to let the water in the system drain out under its own schedule as if we should have, we would not have been so stressed or had to work so hard. Bottom line of course is how much money we could have saved the customer by allowing residual drainage time. Not to mention they acted as if they were going to kick our butts. They were angry at first, but after they understood what was happening and what to expect they became one of our very best customers who also directed us to other great accounts and relationships with other good customers.

You will face challenges like this and in hindsight, it's always easy to see mistakes, but let's try to prevent situations that cause unnecessary work or high costs. Even though a residual leak is active due to natural process such as heat, pressure as no new water is being added. These processes are actually natural processes.

Many customers have been impressed with my insight because we told him to be patient, and let nature take its course and allow the roof to drain its excessive water. They did, the roof stopped leaking and its lead to much more work.

You would be surprised how much pressure can be put on a roof surface from a heavy rain. If a rain event is heavier than usual, this to will cause an old roof leak to reactivate. This can be determined by the color of the water. If the water looks dirty, rusty it maybe very old, probably residual. If the water is clear, it usually means fresh or new. Understand that weight of heavy rain or water will also cause the roof decking to slightly change shape and may cause it to slope differently, and may cause the water to leak at another location close by that has never leaked before. Once the water within the system is not heavy enough to drain out, it will begin the natural evaporation process and all residual activity will stop.

This process of drying roof layer after layer can take months if not years. A rule of thumb is, if a building has good ventilation and circulation, the roof will dry out pretty quick within three months. If the building has poor ventilation and circulation, it may take years for the roof to dry out completely. Of course, all buildings and ventilation systems vary per location.

If you are dealing with what is a pretty major roof leak, always expect some residual drainage. Most of the time when a repair is made and the roof leak stops and its still raining outside, and then you know that the problem has been solved. You may have stopped the active leak, but you have not removed any of the water within the system. Customers are not aware of this fact. Some have asked if we could remove the water in the system. That would take removing the membrane, insulation and removal of the water in the flutes of the decking. Also, replace the wet insulation and the roof membrane in the affected area with new and dry materials. That cost is just too much for some customers, but if that is what the customer wants, you had better do it or they will find someone who will.

Multiple layers of roof will have a much longer drainage rates and may never dry out completely. Cutting off the source of water is the best way to fight back against any future problems.

If you are called back to a roof leak, always think about the possibility of residual drainage. Take a measurement and see for yourself. If the amount draining out is less than previously and is short lived, this means you probably have residual drainage.

A rare residual drainage scenario that will confirm you have a bulls-eye is if you go out on a roof leak call, and the leak is not active and it is not raining. During the search grid process you find an entry point or two and make repairs, suddenly the roof begins leaking, thats a good sign. This means, heat is no longer escaping and warming up moisture within the system in turn expanding and draining out. If this non-active roof related problem activates under these circumstances, be happy you did a good thing. This is very rare, but does happen under the right circumstances. Just make sure you make your customer aware of the circumstances of residual drainage.

Residuals from chapter 10

Residual Drainage is the final amount of excessive water trapped within a roof system that is pushed out under the proper circumstances.

Heat generated by sunshine, or weight from a rain event will often reactive a solved roof related problem.

Residual drainage is usually short lived.

Residual Drainage does not happen on all roofs, but is usually associated with developed roof leaks.

Residual drainage can happen day after day around the warmest part of the day until all the excessive water is drained out. This process in extreme cases may take up to two weeks.

Residual drainage is a natural occurring process that happens under the right circumstances.

It is your responsibility to inform the customer of the possibility of residual drainage.

Let the customer know if their roof leak reactivates, let it finish draining out and complete its task. If the activity is not short lived, you must go out and investigate.

Chapter 20

Isolators

Above one of my most effective inventions. It's called an Isolator. I first began working on it in 1993. We needed to make repairs but under some circumstances, it can become very difficult to complete that task.

Sometimes we have to improvise on the job. Do not look for any help from your office. Besides, this is what they pay you. By that, I mean you have to come up with solutions using what you have on hand. Sometimes, that's tough.

Above we have an old school disc anchor rubber roof with ice, water and mud on the surface. Below we applied my Isolator and removed the water and ice.

Above we have the Isolator in place and the surface is drying out. This gave the customer relief until we could make a better repair. As you can see, it worked great.

Why am I showing you this? This is an example what a repairman can do under extreme circumstances. The company below the roof had already suffered thousands of dollars of ruined merchandise and they need immediate relief.

I hope that you will not have to build an Isolator without warning any time soon. A common problem that we do face during rain events is how to divert water until a repair can be made. Even between raindrops, we sometimes cannot make a temporary repair and are forced to come back later. One thing about temps is that sometime they don't stick very well, and we just have to lower the water level just a little to make a temporary seal.

As long as you have warm temperatures you can just about put down a temp on any type of roof. When the temperature drops down below 40 degrees Fahrenheit or so, it becomes much more difficult to attach the temp to the roof surface.

Since my Isolator will not be available to the public until July 2014, you will have to rely on what you have on hand. We for the most part carry around rags and lap sealant in our vans/work trucks as standard with required work items. We can still make an isolator that we can use to make a temporary repair and in some cases a permanent repair. Things don't always work out for us, but the more effort you put into it the more positive output you can get back out of it. Anyway, it can't hurt to try new things. Heck, sometimes they work!

Above we have a typical re-enforced rubber roof directly after a rain with drizzle falling intermittent. No matter what type of Lap Sealant you have, here are the basic applications. Special note: Some lap sealants are better than others at this particular application. I would recommend one over all because of their excellent qualities but we have not asked or will not ask for permission to do so in this field guide.

We had a leak over a clothing store and it was driving their manager crazy. Despite heavy humidity and light to medium rain events, we pushed the envelope. First, we located the area above.

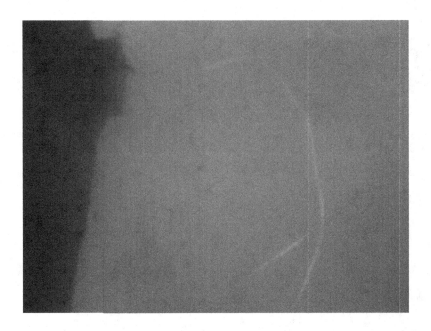

Above we have a semi-blurry picture of our Entry point. Sorry it's blurry, this was caused by the high humidity and dew points. We dried it off repeatedly with rags but every time we started to put down any type of temp, it would start sprinkling and did so all day before we got there, and after we left.

Photo above shows the rain/light sprinkles that interrupted our attempt to make a temp. The roof was on a slope so we only needed a Half Moon Isolator. Yes, you can make temporary Isolators out of lap sealant, like in the picture below.

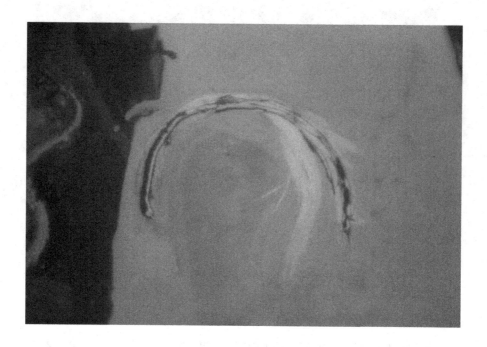

We were able to make a temp and stop the activity. Matter of fact, we removed the bucket and opened the isle for the manager. While we were confirming the leak had subsided and cleaned up, the manager came back and was stunned to see that the leak completely stopped.

He told us that all flat roofs leak and there is nothing you can do about it. He was an older guy and apparently had low expectations. Maybe that's just the way his previous roof repairmen lead him to believe. Needless to say, we picked up the entire shopping center. Those repairmen eventually faded away.

They couldn't compete against us. Look, no matter what happens, whether you stop the leak or not, your company is going to send them a bill, if nothing else at least for the service call. Those guys depended on repeat leaks and this particular leak had been active for three years. We show up out of nowhere and stop the leak, even if only temporarily within 45 minutes under very difficult circumstances.

The point here is to be able to help someone in the moment of need. The clothing store really needed some help. After the leak was stopped and the isle was cleaned up, the manager's demeanor completely changed. He went from mister pissed off to mister wonderful and charming. This is what it is all about people. Roof repair work sucks. It really does, mainly because of the weather conditions and heavy materials, pushing water and shoveling gravel and the pay isn't that great either. Why do we do it? You know why, because this is the type of person you are. You have to be willing to take those chances and go the extra mile. Without an Isolator we would not have had the temp to work as well as it did.

Sometimes the water is very deep you have to lay down a complete circle. You should be able to dry up the center with rags and using only the lap caulk as a mini isolator.

Some roofing companies won't take advantage of this opportunity. They insist on that second call back money. Temporary Isolators can be V-shaped with the arrow pointing upward toward the slope, like an arrow tip. Sometimes you have to add two temporary isolators. First one to slow down the initial flow enough to get a smaller but more effective Isolator in place below the first one.

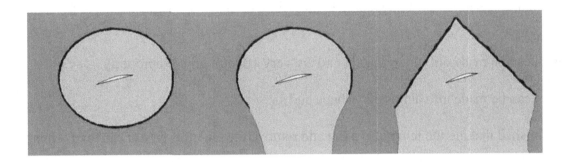

We have the Full Circle, Half Moon and Arrow Head temporary Isolators. They will serve you well when needed.

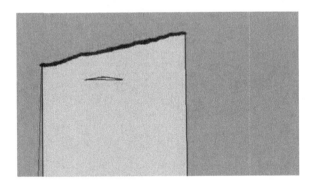

Isolators do not have to be round. Sometimes you only need to put down a sloped Isolator. This will divert the water away long enough to get a decent temp on the surface.

The cleaner the surface the better the Isolator will perform. If at all possible try to wipe the area as clean as possible with rags and then you can apply your lap sealant with a lot less effort.

This is just another opportunity in your toolbox of possibilities. Not everything goes to plan; any help is big help when needed. When lap sealant refuses to stick because of water and cool temperatures, Isolators will give you a little more of an advantage.

Residuals from chapter 20

Isolators are designed to give the repairman a window to make a repair, whether that is temporary or permanent repair requirement.

Factory made Isolators are not available to the public until 2013, so you will have to make your own.

Isolators can be made out of lap sealant and are very effect if applied properly.

Isolators can be made into almost any shape and size.

When finished making the temp, use a rag and remove the Isolator, or you can do it when you return.

Temporary Isolators are usually either, Half Moon, Arrow Head, or Full Circle and Sloped Diverter shapes.

Isolators can be applied on Built-Up roofs utilizing good quality roof cement.

Chapter 21

Protecting Yourself

Everything so far in this field guide has dealt with everything and everyone else for the most part except us. What about us? How do we protect our selves as far as being a Roof Repairman or Repair Specialist?

As you may already know, it is very easy to get into all kinds of trouble on the roof. Heck, there are just as many ways to get in trouble on the roof than off the roof. Thinking back to all of the problems, disasters and aggravation, suffering that most of us have gone through without really needing to be over whelming. How most of us survive is a mystery when you think about it.

You probably remember at the beginning of this book we talked about not getting involved in something without any proof. For instance, how we never tell on any one on the roof unless either we have witnesses or pictures in case there is damage that someone has to pay for. You can get your ass sued off if you're not careful. Again, be careful of what you speak of or speak about because it may haunt you in a legal way.

How quickly we can get in trouble by gossiping goes without saying. Protect yourself, no gossiping. No opinion about anything or anyone. Professionals have nothing to do with gossip. It's hurtful and juvenile and could cost you your job.

Never have seen an accident that was caused by drugs or alcohol. I did see accidents that were caused by stupidity. Fact is it's hard to put up with daily sunburns, chemical exposure, Pitch and Emulsions and the sheer hard work and heavy labor that go into even the smallest repair. Take aspirin when need if allowed by your doctor and drink plenty of water, it helps tremendously.

I've learned to wear sunscreen, and how to divide the work so one person isn't doing everything while the other watches. Cutting down on exposure to chemicals and eating properly and getting enough sleep replaces the need for alcohol and drugs. Many wonderful years clean and sober for myself. Others unfortunately haven't been so fortunate. The downward spiral of drug use is usually devastating and even fatal for a typical roofer, repairman or woman, please I beg you don't do that.

Let's talk about other protection. Our work environment usually is pretty rotten. You know the drill, starts raining, you get a call and have to head out in the rain, snow or extreme heat to freezing cold temperatures.

How we dress makes a big difference in the quality of our day, our attitude and quality of our work. It's a wonder how some of us survive the weather. Have you ever forgotten to put on long johns in the morning when you are dressed and had to freeze your ass off all day? Yeah, we do that. We can't do anything about a bad memory except try harder next time but you can protect yourself when you dress appropriately.

Glasses

Prescription glasses or contacts if needed should always be worn when searching out a roof leak. Besides, there is a chance we might over look a roof related problem even with perfect eye site. Do yourself a favor and wear your glass or contacts if prescribed, it can save you a lot of heartache.

Sun glasses/Safety glasses

Use to be a day when you had to wear either clear safety glasses or sunglasses. Now we have the safety sunglass combination that is cheap and safe. Always have sunglasses or tinted safety glasses on your person at all times.

Different colored safety glasses will show details that you cannot see under normal circumstance. For instance, yellow safety glasses show more wear and tear through traffic on the roof the typical safety glasses. If you do have multiple colored safety glasses, switch them out and look at the roof. You would be amazed at what they can show you.

Hats

Wear some kind of hat to protect the top of your head and face from gamma rays or sunshine and sunburn. In the winter, a huge amount of heat is lost from the top of the head. You have two arms, two legs and only one head. Take care of it!

Gloves

Always wear gloves when working with chemicals and heavy or sharp items. In wintertime, we often have to go without gloves to do detail or handle tech screws and will often leave them off. Wear your gloves as much as possible. They prevent chemical exposure and arthritis. Not to mention preventing different types of nail fungus.

Clothing

Black colored clothing in the winter protects more from hypothermia.

White clothing for the summer protects you more from heat exhaustion.

Most repairmen and helpers will have an overnight bag to carry with them in their work vehicle. In case there is an emergency and you have to stay over night, it can save a lot of time when it comes to those last minute emergencies.

Some companies may require you to wear a uniform. For those people who don't have to work 15 stories up in high winds, you don't know what its like, uniforms suck! Typical uniforms are good for people who work in factories or less evasive service jobs. For roofers and repairmen, they are too hot in the summer time and lack flexibility.

Uniforms are also almost useless in the wintertime. I've challenged many bosses over the years about wearing polyester uniforms. When it's in the middle of winter with the high, winds and frigid temperatures forget about it. You can refuse based on safety issues. Hypothermia is serious. If you are working for someone who is more concerned about their image more than your health, there is something wrong.

Boots

Do not spend two hundred dollars on the most expensive work boots. No matter how well they are made, or how so called water proof/water resistant they are, take it from someone who wasted the money and found within three weeks, water was seeping in at the toes. Cheaper and better to simply buy the inexpensive work boots and wear a pair of galoshes or rubbers over top of the work boots. The galoshes will last a long time too.

During cold temperatures, don't wear more than two pairs of socks. What will happen, is that your feet will begin to sweat, then your feet get very cold and feel like solid blocks of ice. Some people wear multiple pairs of socks because of the cold. What they don't realize, is once your feet become wet from excessive sweating they get just as cold as if you had no socks on at all.

Do not over tighten the strings on your boots. You want the heat within your boot to escape out of the top of the boot to cut down on sweating and to minimize athletes foot.

Tools

It is your responsibility to have all needed hand tools.

There is a specific list of what tools you will need from my list, but there is also a minimum amount of tools you will also need that may be required by your company. Some companies will not let you work unless you have the required minimum amount of tools.

All companies have some type of list of what those are. Collect them and keep them close. Do not loan them out to anyone other than your foreman/supervisor or helper, ever.

Water

This is one of those necessities that many be easily over looked. Some will bring a long a soda and expect it to get them by. On a hot day, my four staff crew would drink empty two five-gallon size coolers of water within an eight-hour day and still be dehydrated.

If you urinate and it's a yellow colored, you are not drinking enough water. You should pee clear. That is the only true sign that you are properly hydrated.

Food and Drinks

Now are you going to tell us what to eat? Probably what you are wondering, and yes there are foods that are good for roofers. Because roofers and repair people burn an incredible amount of energy and deal with extreme heat there are foods to avoid while working on the roof, and other foods that are good for the roof top.

Milk and Dairy products are not good for people working in extreme heat. They can make us sick, nauseous and can create down time situations.

Stay away from hot foods in the summer time. Cold cuts, fruits and vegetable are the best any time in warm or summer months.

Try not to consumer too much caffeine. A little caffeine goes a long way.

No alcoholic beverages anytime summer or winter on the roof. Sport drinks are also a waste of money. Pure, clean water is the best way to prevent dehydration. Of course, water does not have calories.

Stay away from cold drinks and refreshments in the wintertime. Warm meals, soup and hot sandwiches are idea for wintertime.

Again, take it easy on the caffeine. Above all, do drink water, even in the winter. You run a higher risk of dehydration in the wintertime than you do in the summer time. That is because, when its cold outside we often think were not thirsty, just cold. Cold air is drier than warm air and dehydration is usually over looked or ignored during winter or cold temperatures.

In addition, for heavens sakes try to stay away from bars, and criminal type activity when out of town. Cannot even begin the list the men who were shot, killed or sent to jail just because they were associated with a place or group of people who went innocently to a bar for a beer. If you want to have a drink, that's fine. Unfortunately, some of us go over board and suffer for it the rest of our lives, not counting the next day. The real crime is, when an employee is recovering from a big drunk on the roof, everyone else has to carry their ass. It's a quick way to get kicked off a crew, take it easy.

Residuals from chapter 21

Always wear safety glass when on the roof, any roof.

Some colored safety glasses such as yellow, red and blue can show wear and tear on the roof that is not normally seen.

Wear a hat in the summer to protect your scalp from the sun, and cover your head in the winter to minimize heat loss.

Wear black or dark color clothing in the winter and white or light colored clothing in the summer.

Always wear work boots, and keep a pair of galoshes for deep water.

All employees should have their own tools and hand tools.

Drink plenty of water, no alcohol or high sugar soft drinks.

Never use drugs before during or around any roof job.

Take it easy on the caffeine.

Eat foods that will not make you sick such as dairy products in the hot summer time or ice cream in the winter time.

Avoid problem areas, and new places/bars or pubs to avoid trouble when out of town.

Glossary

Activity

The physical identification of an active leak or leaking.

Accident

An event that happens completely by chance, with no planning or deliberate intent.

Proper Search Techniques

Proper Search Techniques begins with collecting good information such as measurements and activity information. This also includes, I.T.I., Water Testing with Time Differentials, Trough Search and Perpendicular and Parallel Strategies. Sound Resonance, Piggybacking, and Paths of Travel are also part of these techniques.

Application

The relevance or value that something has, especially when it is applied to a specific field or area.

Ballast

Ballast is a loosely laid layer of gravel that is utilized to hold a roof down.

Ballasted Roof

Usually an EPDM or built-up roof will have gravel of different sizes on the top surface to stabilize and protect the roof surface from possible damage or from being blown off.

Basic Construction

The practice of standard construction applications.

Bi-Directional decking

Bi-directional decking is a term utilized to describe metal decking installed on the same building that runs in two different directions.

Bitumen

A sticky mixture of hydrocarbons found in substances such as asphalt and tar. Source: petroleum.

Built-Up Roof

Built up roofs differ, usually Bitumen or asphalt applied over insulation with layers of either paper or fiberglass roll material. Most torch down applications utilizes bitumen as the main product.

Business

A company or other organization that buys and sells goods, makes products, or provides services.

Career

A job or occupation regarded as a long-term or lifelong activity.

Chiller

Slang for a large air-cooled water circulation system utilized to cool large work areas such as factories or where large groups of people work.

Collateral Damage

Unintended damage to civilian life or property during an operation or service.

Commonalities

Shared characteristic or quality.

Commercial and Industrial

Non-residential or pertaining to factories or manufacturing facilities.

Crew

Two or more people working together to complete a task.

Customer

A person or company that buys goods or services.

Corrugated Decking

Typical metal decking that is utilized with a bottom flute and an upper rib. This decking is attached to supports and I beams while the roof is attached mechanically or weighed down by a ballast system.

Cross Lateral Circulation

Cross Lateral Circulation is the technical term for liquid traveling from one side to the other side.

Cubic Centimeter

A single drop of fluid is a cubic centimeter. Typical raindrop is also a cubic centimeter. Unusual rain events produce droplets larger and small than a cubic centimeter.

Curb

Usually a four sided metal or wooden box with a flange on the bottom to anchor through and a wood nailer on top lip. Curbs support units, mechanical applications.

Element

A separate identifiable part of something, or a distinct group within a larger group.

Entry Point

An Entry point can be a slice, cut or hole and even a rip or some type of opening that allows water into the roof surface some how.

EPDM

Rubber product used to cover the surface of a roof, manufactured by several rubber producing companies all over the world.

Eye Witness

Somebody who sees occurrence: somebody who gives evidence after seeing or hearing something.

Evidence

Something that gives a sign or proof of the existence or truth of something, or that helps somebody to come to a particular conclusion.

False Positive

A roof related process or test that appears to be positive but is in fact erroneous.

Field Guide

An illustrated manual that is used to identify objects, processes, or applications, problems and solutions in their natural habitats

Flashing

Many types of flashing exist. Metal flashing which tie in building to roof applications. Flashing can also be an uncured rubber applied to specific design areas intended for custom use.

Flat Roof

The most typical roof utilized by most factories, companies and businesses. This roof can be sloped, barreled or angled and still be considered a flat roof.

Flute

Bottom half of corrugated metal decking.

Foreman

Man or woman in charge of other workers: who is in charge of a group of other workers, e.g. on a construction site or in a factory.

Fork Lift

A four-wheel vehicle utilized in many companies, factories and warehouses to move heavy or large amounts of material or product. Usually move the products around on wooden skids.

Gas Mileage

The amount of miles traveled in relation to gas or fuel used. Most repair crews have to keep track of their gas mileage.

Generic

Applying to any member of a group or class that are, over all similar.

Gravel

Small stones: small stones used for paths or for making concrete.

Heat Weld System

Heat weld systems are generally manufactured from PVC type materials and constructed with heat guns and hard rollers as well as prefabricated corners and flashings.

Helper

To make it easier or possible for somebody to do something that one person cannot do alone by providing assistance.

Hole

A gap or opening in or through something. In roofing, it is an entry point.

Hours Worked

Hours worked is an account of time spent on a particular job, day or week.

H.V.A.C. Unit

Heating, Ventilation and Air Conditioning, or HVAC.

Indicators

Something that shows what conditions are: something observed or calculated that is used to show the presence or state of a condition or trend.

Installation

The action of applying or installing materials or attaching materials to some type of substrate. Usually a construction requirement.

Insulation

Insulation is made from all types of material such as fiberglass, recycled paper and biodegradable and non-biodegradable material such as Styrofoam. Insulation is used to keep heating and cooling costs down by laying it on a buildings top surface before the roof is applied over top of it.

Internal Thermal Identification

Identifying Entry points, holes with the assistance of moisture trapped inside a roof system that heats up and expands outwards back out of an Entry point.

Isolator

Isolators are a temporary dam utilized to provide dry working conditions for applying permanent patches.

Lap

A typical lap is where you join or mate two separate pieces of material with heat/chemicals to complete a watertight seal, making the roof watertight.

Leak

Slang, used to identify water draining from the ceiling level or anything that inadvertently drains fluids of some type.

Legitimate

Conforming to acknowledged standards: complying with recognized rules, standards, or traditions.

Macro-Entry Point

A Marco-Entry point is the description of a large opening in the membrane, usually beyond 100 feet in length.

Manufacturers Suggested Recommendations

Specific way of accomplishing a task that must be conformed to by the applicator for the benefit of the over all task.

Map

Discover and show something: to discover something and create a visual representation of it.

Material

Usually indicates the type of membrane or what type of material the roof has been manufactured from.

Mechanical Fastener

Basically metal screws. Mechanical fasteners come in all sizes and types. They are utilized as a means of attachment when apply a roof over a metal or wood type deck.

Membrane

A thin, pliable, and often porous sheet of any natural or artificial material.

Metric

Relating to metric system: relating to or using the metric system of measurement.

Micro Entry Point

Very small Entry cut, hole. These Entry points are usually about an eighth in diameter.

Multi-layered Roof

Two or more roofs installed on top of each other.

Multi-Directional decking

This description for decking runs more than two directions on the same building and under the same roof.

Negative

Logic opposing: denying or contradicting a statement, proof, or argument.

Negative Static Pressure

Negative static pressure can cause a roof to pull in more than average amount of water through a system. If you have a small pinhole in a valley area that holds water, you can get large amounts of water if negative pressure is in control of the building.

Non-Typical Roof Leak

Non-typical roof leak is when an Exit point and Entry point exceed thirty feet and beyond. Non-typical roof leaks can travel hundreds of feet, but usually with in the same flute in metal decking.

Other Sources

Other Sources are items that are not roof related that cause leaks that mimic roof leaks. Penetrations, Stacks, drains, sprinkler systems, windows, brick and mortar walls are all considered other sources and/or non roof related problems.

Patch

Something that covers or mends: a piece of material used to cover, strengthen, or mend a hole in something.

Piggybacking

Piggybacking is when water travels over tapered insulation or insulation that is kicked tight by installers during installation. Water can run across the top surface of insulation carrying water in what is also called a secondary path of travel.

Positive

Sure: certain and not in doubt.

Positive Static Pressure

The positive static pressure effect happens when you have so much positive pressure in the building that water entering through openings in the membrane is slowed down by air under pressure. Even if you have a larger than average hole in a valley area, you may only get a small amount of water.

Porous State

A porous state is an area of rubber membrane more than 12 inches by 12 inches that may have many small micro holes.

Probe

Small piece of metal or plastic approx. 6 to 8 inches in length and about an eight of an inch in diameter. Often old discarded welding rods will be made into probes. Probes are utilized for insertion into small Entry points to track water intake.

Problem

Puzzle to be solved: a question or puzzle that needs to be solved.

Process

Series of actions: a series of actions directed toward a specific aim.

Process of Elimination

Where a person or persons eliminate one problem at a time or during each visit.

Productive

Producing much: producing something abundantly and efficiently.

Professional Manner

The skill, competence, or character expected of a member of a highly trained profession.

Public Relations

Promotion of favorable image: the practice or profession of establishing, maintaining, or improving a favorable relationship between an institution or person and the public.

Quality

The highest or finest standard (*often used before a noun*) *quality products*.

Rain Event

Rain Event is proper grammar for any type of rain. If it were a thunderstorm, one would say, "It was an extreme rain event." If you have light rain the night before you would say, "We only had a light rain event last night."

Repair

Fix or mend something: to restore something broken or damaged to good condition.

Repair Foreman

The person who is in control of the roof repair process on site and with the customer.

Repair Technician

Another label or name for a repairman.

Repeat Roof Leak

A repeat roof leak is a roof related problem that has been active more than two times. Residual drainage can mimic an active roof leak, that's why we have to allow sometime and or rain events to push out residual moisture out of the system before it can be categorized as a repeat roof leak.

Residual drainage

Residual drainage can only happen after a roof leak has been repaired and the water stopped. Residual drainage is a result of water trapped in the system that with the force of gravity and heat in combination with pressure reactive a roof leak.

Rib

The tops of metal decking are referred to as ribs.

Roof

Upper covering of building: the outside covering of the top of a building, or the framework supporting this.

Roof Leak

This is where water enters the roof surface or membrane. After water enters the roof membrane, it travels across or around insulation onto decking. Only when water begins draining out of an Exit point do we have a true roof leak/legitimate roof leak.

Roof Related Problem

Roof related problem can a cut or hole in the roof membrane or a penetration leak, wall or mortar absorption, sprinklers, or plumbing leak. All items are covered under this description if they originate above head from the ceiling area.

Roof Repair

Repair made over, or on a roof in hopes to stop a roof related problem such as a roof leak.

Roof Repair Specialist

A repair specialist who understands all processes, and applications as it relates to roof related problems and their possible solutions with a success rate of 95% or higher.

Rules

Principles governing conduct an authoritative principle set forth to guide behavior or Action.

Search

Discover something by examination: to discover, come to know, or find something by Examination.

Search Area

Search areas outline the parameters of a complete and thorough investigation. Angle of the insulation, decking and type of roof dictate where a search area begins and ends.

Siphoning Effect

The Siphoning effect happens when water over flows metal barriers or wall to point to where the water will pull additional drops or cc is in an intermittent fashion. This type of activity will drip out many drips at one quick burst, then not drip again.

Situation

A particular set of circumstances existing in a particular place or at a particular time.

Solution

A way of resolving difficulty: a method of successfully dealing with a problem or difficulty.

Spider Webbing

Spider webbing can happen several ways, a large area of insulation becomes extremely saturated and water is able to spread out across boards of insulation and run across and out of metal decking at 5 or more close locations.

Strategy

A carefully devised plan of action to achieve a goal, or the art of developing or carrying out such a plan.

Success

Achievement of intention: the achievement of something planned or attempted.

Surgical Intervention

When no Entry points are found during an analysis of the roof membrane, and all other procedures have failed, Surgical Intervention is a good candidate to positively identify a problem. This is done by physically opening the roof with a sharp tool, and tracking staining, damaged insulation or rusted decking. With this process, you can physically see the internal workings of your roof related problem. Always make sure you have the right type and amount of materials to return the roof in a warranted state.

Tenant

Occupier of place: somebody living in or on a property.

Theory

Rules and techniques: the body of rules, ideas, principles, and techniques that applies to a subject, especially when seen as distinct from actual practice.

Torch Down Roof

Torch down roofs are generally asphalt based that can be applied over many layers with a top granulated sheet or a finish sheet.

Touchy feely

Touchy feely is an expression for physically touching and pulling flashing and laps in different directions with material in hopes to discover and Entry point. Simply looking at the material is not enough in some cases to expose unseen Entry points.

Trade

Occupation: a skilled occupation, usually one requiring manual labor.

Training

Acquiring of skill: the process of teaching or learning a skill or job.

Trough

Sunken area: a long hollow area in the surface of the ground or the sea bed, or between waves.

Troughing

Troughing is a phenomenon that happens when insulation gets wet due to a cut or slice, hole in roof membrane. Areas could look like ponds, even though there is no water in the pond. Troughing is easy to identify due to dirty, debris and bio decay staining.

Trough Search

Searching across the surface of the roof in hopes of discovering soft or wet insulation that may indicate an entry point near by.

Typical Roof Leak

A typical roof leak will always have the Entry point and Exit point placed or spaced within a 30-foot parameter.

Water Mark

Slang for height of water level on a roof. The height of the water on the roof can be found by dirt/oil etc., residue on wall flashings, penetrations. Watermarks can also lay flat similar to rings in a tree identifying different or varying types of rain events. In some cases, these watermarks copy annually and remain the lifetime of the roof.

Water Testing

Water testing is necessary when no other recourse. After visual and physical searches net no answers, water testing may be necessary. Water testing is essentially flooding the roof from its lowest point upward to its highest point.

Water Testing with Time Differentials

Water testing with time differentials is a secure way of insisting water into a problem area. At each level of a water test, a minimum of fifteen minutes is required as to mimic time for an average rain event.

Weather Condition

The current outside environment as it relates to temperature, humidity and the chance of rain.

Weeping Lap

Weeping lap is a lap that allows water to enter for lack of adhesive or has begun to fail.

Work Vehicle

The company vehicle provided to its employees to carry around materials and to run repairs. Work vehicles should always be clean, tuned up and pass all road safety standards.

About the Author

J. L. Foster hails from Dayton Ohio. John is an accomplished musician who found time to build robots and fly planes. Besides being a huge history buff, John enjoys playing classical guitar, violin and piano.